RANDOM HOUSE
–GOLF–
CROSSWORDS

ISBN 0-8129-3396-6

Random House Puzzles & Games Website Address:
www.puzzlesatrandom.com

Page design and typography by Mark Frnka
Manufactured in the United States of America
4   6   8   9   7   5
First Edition

SPECIAL SALES

Random House Puzzles & Games books are available at special
discounts for bulk purchases for sales promotions or premiums. Special
editions, including personalized covers, excerpts of existing books, and
corporate imprints, can be created in large quantities for special needs.
For more information, contact Random House
Special Markets at 800-800-3246.

RANDOM HOUSE
-GOLF-
CROSSWORDS

STANLEY NEWMAN

**Random House
Puzzles & Games**

1

ACROSS

1 Taxis
5 Family members
9 Tway of the PGA
12 Lopsided win
13 Biblical boat builder
14 Before, in poems
15 Firestone Country Club site
17 Singer __ King Cole
18 Senior golfer Casper
19 Openwork fabric
21 Catch sight of
24 Pleasure boat
27 Mac
30 Slangy suffix
32 Breakfast order
33 Mimic
35 Your and my
36 Armed conflicts
37 __ Maria Olazábal
38 Something simple
40 After deduction of handicap
41 Poker payments
43 Day of the PGA
45 Something indistinct
47 High-minded
51 Caribbean, for example
53 Mashie-niblick
56 Mr. Nagle
57 Head covering
58 Farm storage building
59 Jeff Sluman's home: Abbr.
60 Brainstorm
61 Affirmative votes

DOWN

1 Complainer
2 Senior golfer from Japan
3 Folk singer Ives
4 Fur coat
5 Letters on a telephone
6 Reaction to a hole-in-one
7 Impair
8 Pro-shop buy
9 *Follow the Sun* subject
10 "Are you a man __ mouse?"

1	2	3	4		5	6	7	8	9	10	11
12					13				14		
15				16					17		
18						19		20			
			21		22	23		24			25	26
27	28	29		30			31		32		
33			34		35				36		
37					38		39		40		
41				42		43			44		
		45			46			47		48	49	50
51	52			53		54	55				
56				57				58			
59				60				61			

11 $5 Nassau, for instance

16 Wall Street organization: Abbr.

20 Whole bunch

22 Group on tour

23 Like many U.S. Amateur champs

25 Mean person

26 Attention-getting sound

27 Region south of San Diego

28 Very familiar with

29 Type of tournament

31 Vocal

34 Movie-film holder

39 Arnold Palmer's birthplace: Abbr.

42 Fish dish

44 Uproarious

46 Enjoy a book

48 French cheese

49 Singer Falana

50 Genesis character

51 Aspen gear

52 Electric fish

54 Compete

55 Historical period

ACROSS

1 TV newsman Huntley
5 Tiger Woods' home: Abbr.
8 Male deer
12 Solitary
13 Sleep phenomenon: Abbr.
14 Scorecard-signing place
15 Golf-rules organization: Abbr.
16 Davis Love __
17 Nevada city
18 Fairway material
21 Ryder Cup team
22 French assent
23 Rabbit of kiddie lit
26 Electronic detection device
30 Sushi-bar selection
31 Chicken __ king
32 Rosebush eater
36 Personify
39 Jogged
40 Byron Nelson Classic month
41 Duffer's typical scores
47 Gator's relative
48 In the past
49 *Andy Griffith Show* kid
50 Plumbing problem
51 Tournament sponsors: Abbr.
52 '99 Ryder Cup month: Abbr.
53 Extremely
54 Road curve
55 Former New York Jets owner

DOWN

1 Country __
2 Fireman's need
3 MIT graduate: Abbr.
4 Play together
5 When PGA tournaments' second round is played
6 *Star Wars* princess
7 Friends, to Ballesteros

8 Muscle mishap

9 Pro-shop buys

10 Columnist Landers et al.

11 Sports-car initials

19 Battleship letters

20 Regret

23 Winter-rules month: Abbr.

24 Senior golfer with "fleas"

25 Bullfight cheer

27 __ Paulo, Brazil

28 Ancient

29 Mr. Floyd

33 Like some short putts

34 Once around the track

35 Tie your shoes

36 Decorate leather

37 One-time Chinese chairman

38 "My goodness!"

41 Fairway obstacle, at times

42 Crowd sound

43 Swelled heads

44 Fencing sword

45 Putting jitters

46 Complete collections

47 155, in old Rome

3

ACROSS

1 FDR's dog
5 Actress Gardner
8 Allows
12 G.I.'s offense: Abbr.
13 Place for a kid to sit
14 Spiny houseplant
15 PGA Championship winner in '65
17 Golf organization founded in 1894: Abbr.
18 Symbol of 25 Down
19 "Fore!" is one
20 Neighborhoods
21 Herron of the PGA
22 Extinct bird
23 Engrave deeply
26 Chatter
27 Flying saucer: Abbr.
30 LPGA cofounder
34 Urban transportation
35 1997 U.S. Open champ
36 *Othello* villain
37 Mr. Sutton
38 Stephenson of the LPGA
40 Dressed
43 71, at Royal Troon
44 Mature
47 One of the Great Lakes
48 Trevino's nickname
50 Something to mark
51 Pitching stat: Abbr.
52 Roll-call response
53 "__ well that ends well!"
54 First hole of the back nine
55 Change for a five

DOWN

1 Deliberate slice
2 Not at home
3 1997 PGA Championship winner
4 19th-hole order
5 Security device
6 Be inconsistent
7 Month of the Masters: Abbr.
8 Ms. Baugh
9 Otherwise
10 Julius Caesar outfit
11 Bounding mains
16 __ Classic (Glen Day victory in '99)

20 Isao __
21 Definite article
22 Scratch the surface
23 Flow back
24 Greek cross
25 Jack Whitaker's network
26 Scorecard abbreviation
27 Walker Cup dominator
28 Frequent St. Andrews forecast
29 Yoko __
31 Not working, as a car battery
32 Under the weather
33 Relatives
37 Shoe parts
38 Homeland of Jumbo Ozaki
39 Exist
40 Country singer McEntire
41 Kind of vaccine
42 Invoice
43 Unmixed
44 Prayer conclusion
45 *Pretty Woman* star
46 Former spouses
48 Tennis-match unit
49 Sigma preceder

4

ACROSS

1 Alumnus, for short
5 Faxon of the PGA
9 Spy group: Abbr.
12 Evening, on marquees
13 Acting job
14 Site of a former Trevino tattoo
15 Water hazard
16 Right away: Abbr.
17 Sunbeam
18 LPGA stops
21 Seafood serving
22 Score for a 35 Down
23 Shouted
26 Evade
30 Convent resident
31 One __ time (individually)
32 Bob Costas' employer
35 Mental discipline, for a golfer
37 Portion of corn
39 College, for example: Abbr.
40 See 44 Down
45 __ Angeles
46 Singing syllables
47 Neither under nor over par
49 1997 U.S. Open champ
50 Olympic skater Heiden
51 "__ Only Just Begun"
52 Lawyer: Abbr.
53 Television award
54 Made a deliberate hook

DOWN

1 Economic stat: Abbr.
2 Very funny person
3 __ cost (free)
4 Figure out
5 Cattle marking
6 Singer Julius La __
7 San Antonio landmark
8 Rely
9 Pro-shop rental
10 Some nest eggs: Abbr.
11 Ms. Alcott
19 Fishing gear

20 Prefix meaning 48 Down

23 One of Ted Turner's networks

24 __ of the green

25 Corporation designation: Abbr.

27 Prosecutors: Abbr.

28 __ Classic (Senior PGA event)

29 Have dinner

33 __ Aviv

34 Radio star Rudy

35 Duffer's dream

36 Very clever

38 Provide with new weapons

39 U.S. Women's Open champ in '78

40 '50s pro Tommy

41 Aide: Abbr.

42 Svelte

43 Completed

44 With 40 Across, 1988 British Open champ

45 Meadow

48 Innovative

ACROSS

1 Medicine dosages: Abbr.
4 Golf-club part
7 Actress Shire
12 "Bali __"
13 Make a mistake
14 Newsman Sevareid et al.
15 Prepare to hit the ball
17 Ponies up
18 Notions
19 Let in
21 Hurler of seven no-hitters
22 Sponsor of a PGA and senior PGA event
23 Singer Fitzgerald
26 Fictional jungle hero
29 At any time, in poetry
30 Washington city
33 Lion, often
35 Feel poorly
36 All __ (inept)
38 Boast
40 Had lunch
41 Manage somehow
45 Instant-replay technique
47 *Dead __ Perfect* (golf TV movie of '88)
48 Wears
50 Short-game skill
52 Make one's first shot
53 *The Heart __ Lonely Hunter*
54 Neckline shape
55 Golf-shoe needs
56 Behave
57 Superman's insignia

DOWN

1 Office furniture
2 Bag toter
3 Surface of an LP
4 Prepares to 52 Across
5 Hospital areas: Abbr.
6 Synthetic
7 "Us" or "Them"
8 Revered PGA nickname
9 Golfer nicknamed "The Machine"
10 Road hazard

11 Beast of burden
16 Totaled
20 "My goodness!"
22 1979 PGA Championship winner
24 Confederate general
25 Incoming airplane: Abbr.
27 Quantity: Abbr.
28 __ Hill (San Francisco neighborhood)
30 File-folder part
31 Broadcast
32 Word in many golf tournament names
34 Wide tie
37 Ideal place
39 Pro-shop buy
42 Martini ingredient
43 Torrey __
44 Barely beats
46 Wallet contents
47 Scoring average, for one
48 The "good" cholesterol
49 Football coach Parseghian
51 UCLA rival

6

ACROSS
1 That woman
4 Draft organization: Abbr.
7 Texas ___ (putter)
12 Cut (off)
13 "The Raven" writer
14 Opera solos
15 Frozen water
16 Roll after landing
17 Soup server
18 One of the majors
21 ___ jiffy (quickly)
22 Shoe fabrics
26 Prepare to hit the ball
29 Corporate executives: Abbr.
30 Southern state: Abbr.
31 Put on the payroll
32 Sara Lee Classic month
33 One-half of CCCIV
34 Compass point: Abbr.
35 Brent Geiberger, to Al
36 ___ and Ancient Golf Club
37 Increases, as a lead
39 At this moment
40 1999 British Open site
45 Gobbled up
48 Rural hotel
49 Frequently, in poems
50 Mont ___ (French peak)
51 Silent assent
52 Soldiers' hangout: Abbr.
53 Singer/actress Midler
54 Curved letter
55 Director ___ Howard

DOWN
1 Narrow cut
2 1994 Bob Hope champ
3 Fencing blade
4 Leapt up
5 American march composer
6 Mailed away
7 Stadler's nickname

8 Wipe clean
9 Performed
10 Guy's date
11 Language suffix
19 Gold source
20 Take notice of
23 Long-hitting pro
24 Director Kazan
25 Leave port
26 New York Mets' home

27 Factor in club selection
28 Made angry
29 Moving vehicle
32 Secure, as a ship
33 Dairy animals
35 Position at the ball
36 Tournament quartet
38 Aroma

39 Things to avoid
41 Half a round
42 Compete regularly as a pro
43 In that case
44 British prep school
45 Recede
46 Pub serving
47 Sylvester, to Tweety

7

ACROSS

1 Citrus drinks
5 __ Worth (home of Colonial)
9 Radio-station employees: Abbr.
12 Amateur-status definition, for example
13 Pennsylvania port
14 "That's delicious!"
15 1993 Ryder Cup captain
17 Beer relative
18 15 Across' team
19 Golfer with an army
21 Entice
24 Actor Cronyn
26 Long, long __
27 Composer Stravinsky
29 Number of U.S. Opens won by Sam Snead
33 '64 U.S. Open site
36 Russian ruler of yore
37 Close by
38 Civil War side: Abbr.
39 Israeli airline
41 View from Pebble Beach
43 Golfer's practice place
46 Alphabetic trio
47 __ Lanka
48 Golfing groups
54 Singer Damone
55 Not wild
56 Knucklehead
57 LPGA Rookie of the Year in 1998
58 Dirty Harry's employer: Abbr.
59 Cry of pain

DOWN

1 Golfer Wall
2 Twosome
3 Shade tree
4 Make sure of
5 Greek cheese
6 Surgeons' workplaces: Abbr.
7 __ de Janeiro
8 Midmorning
9 Actress Cannon
10 Inkster of the LPGA

11 *Peter Pan* pirate
16 Up and about
20 __-Tahoe Open
21 Diplomacy
22 Self-images
23 "__ Lisa"
24 Golf-club part
25 __ Major (Big Dipper)
28 Actress Rowlands
30 __ upon a time

31 Astronauts' organization
32 Pizazz
34 First name of the Shark
35 Mashies and niblicks
40 Some jabs
42 1971 Masters winner
43 Respond to an invitation

44 Soprano's selection
45 Mr. Faldo
46 '60s talking horse of TV
49 Bumbling sort
50 Diamond arbiter
51 One of the Stooges
52 Right-angle shape
53 Oil additive

8

ACROSS
1 Ritzy
5 Merely
9 Mr. Sutton
12 Syrian, for example
13 __ Aoki
14 Former heavyweight boxing champ
15 6'3" LPGA Hall of Famer
17 Formerly called
18 *Ghostbusters* goo
19 Memorable pirate
21 Defeat in competition
24 Arson is one
27 __ Paulo, Brazil
30 Eastern European
32 Got a hole-in-one
33 Scandinavian capital
35 Trouble
36 Alert
37 Shakespearean king
38 Webster of dictionaries
40 Veggie in a pod
41 Stuns
43 PGA members
45 Endorsement negotiators: Abbr.
47 "Santa __ Is Coming to Town"
51 Hawaiian Ladies Open month: Abbr.
53 1999 U.S. Open site
56 Alias: Abbr.
57 Actor Alda
58 Prefix for bucks
59 __ Aviv
60 Kite's namesakes
61 '50s *Tonight Show* host

DOWN
1 Congressional contributors: Abbr.
2 Evangelist Roberts
3 Dress of India
4 Nuclear weapon
5 Mr. Dent
6 2002 Winter Olympics host
7 Holed a putt
8 Pick-me-up
9 Word on a scorecard

10 British brew
11 Golf ball's position
16 Trevino et al.
20 Create a caricature
22 Darned, as a sock
23 Army group
25 Unimportant
26 Author Ferber
27 Real-estate sign
28 On a cruise ship, perhaps
29 1999 Masters champ
31 The Golden __ (Nicklaus)
34 Western state: Abbr.
39 Scott of the PGA
42 March honoree
44 Poor-playing streak
46 Grain-storage place
48 Vicinity
49 It maintains Golf House: Abbr.
50 Woods or Els
51 Bad way to hit a ball
52 __ out a living
54 *Platoon* setting
55 Naval Academy graduate: Abbr.

9

ACROSS

1 Aid in wrongdoing
5 Pharmaceutical regulator: Abbr.
8 __ Forest (alma mater of 18 Across)
12 Hit a ball deep into a bunker
13 Foursome in Monopoly: Abbr.
14 Nautical adverb
15 __-a-brac
16 Clock numeral
17 Vex
18 Winner of 60 PGA tournaments
21 Huge
22 After taxes
23 Trinket
26 African desert
30 Important asset for a golfer
31 Power source
32 Type of milk
36 Deep cuts
39 Where Medinah is: Abbr.
40 Chip shot's path
41 Type of tournament
47 Where Nicklaus was born
48 Belly muscles
49 Nevada city
50 Church receptacle
51 Massage
52 Preceding nights
53 Gorillas
54 Pig's place
55 Makes a dress

DOWN

1 Eban of Israel
2 Hamilton's duel opponent
3 Ireland
4 Babe Ruth contemporary
5 Place to keep things cool
6 Faucet flaw
7 Chinese and Koreans
8 What a fireplace provides
9 Lotion additive
10 Actor Dullea

11 Snakelike fish
19 __ *Abner*
20 Grazing area
23 Place for clubs
24 Ventilate
25 Actress Thurman
27 Fireplace remains
28 Feel sorry about
29 Response: Abbr.

33 They should be replaced on a course
34 Inventor Whitney
35 Church platforms
36 F. Scott Fitzgerald character
37 Onassis' nickname

38 Leader-board postings
41 Flapjack franchise's initials
42 Back __
43 Be next to
44 Actress Campbell
45 All over again
46 Defeat
47 Ghost __ chance

10

ACROSS
1 Chip or putt
5 Mr. Wargo
8 Pocket-watch pockets
12 Lubricates
13 Santa __, Calif.
14 Swear
15 Alternate-year golf event
17 Actress Olin
18 Part of a sock
19 Distress signal
20 Computer option
21 Dollar fractions: Abbr.
22 Money player
23 In addition
26 Highway warning sign
27 Scrooge comment

30 1994 Solheim Cup team member
34 Hardwood tree
35 Winter bug
36 West Point team
37 On vacation
38 Golfer Nagle
40 Mr. Wadkins
43 __ moment (very soon)
44 __ alai
47 Medicinal plant
48 Where golf was born
50 Waiter's handout
51 Permit
52 Poker ritual
53 Slightest sound
54 Scorecard abbreviation
55 Phoenix suburb

DOWN
1 Alphabetize
2 "__ Silver, away!"
3 Ye __ Tea Shoppe
4 Mao __-tung
5 Mexican snacks
6 Responsibility
7 Tourist's reference
8 1990 PGA Player of the Year
9 Having a + on the scoreboard
10 Cher's one-time partner
11 Did the backstroke
16 Q followers
20 Dangerous reptile

Grid numbers visible: 1, 2, 3, 4, 5, 6, 7, 8, 9, 10, 11, 12, 13, 14, 15, 16, 17, 18, 19, 20, 21, 22, 23, 24, 25, 26, 27, 28, 29, 30, 31, 32, 33, 34, 35, 36, 37, 38, 39, 40, 41, 42, 43, 44, 45, 46, 47, 48, 49, 50, 51, 52, 53, 54, 55

21 Portable bed
22 U.N. observer group: Abbr.
23 Hubbub
24 Mauna __
25 It may be common or preferred: Abbr.
26 Dallas school: Abbr.
27 "It's cold!"
28 Point at the target
29 Attention-getting shout
31 Problematical
32 Santa's helper
33 *2001* computer
37 Match play victory margin, at times
38 Wind-speed unit
39 Have a snack
40 Night-table topper
41 Ship captain's order
42 __ of the above
43 On the rocks
44 Ms. Blalock
45 Picnic pests
46 Inspiration
48 Crafty
49 On the __ (fleeing)

11

ACROSS

1 Majestic in scope
5 __ Maria Olazábal
9 Bradley of the LPGA
12 Gossip columnist Barrett
13 Abba of Israel
14 Garden tool
15 Hill-building insects
16 Lounge around
17 Country rest stop
18 Gene Sarazen's most famous shot
21 Ms. Alcott
22 __ Classic (April PGA tourney)
23 Mexican entrée
26 Vote in
30 Performer's acknowledgment
31 Canine foot
32 #3 wood
35 African nation
37 Fish eggs
39 MGM's mascot
40 Winner of 11 straight tournaments in '45
45 Luau side dish
46 Sketch
47 Leader-board word
49 Swiss mountain
50 Centers of activity
51 *Doctor Zhivago* role
52 ACLU concern: Abbr.
53 Ems' preceders
54 Pigeonhole

DOWN

1 Historical period
2 Water hazard
3 Obsessed by
4 __ water
5 Toast topping
6 Woodwind instrument
7 Winston-__, N.C.
8 Close up one's shoes
9 Mr. Mickelson
10 Top-rated
11 First hole of the back nine
19 ASCAP rival
20 Senior golfer Morgan

23 NBC rival
24 Fairway bounce
25 __ Jima
27 Ecology agency: Abbr.
28 Is able to
29 U.S. Airways competitor
33 Hockey great Bobby
34 Chicken __ soup
35 Type of toothpaste
36 Golf-club parts
38 Sign up
39 Clark's exploration partner
40 Tommy "Thunder" __
41 Nervousness on the green
42 Table salt's chemical symbol
43 Racetrack's shape
44 Infamous Roman emperor
45 70, at Shinnecock Hills
48 Natalie Cole's dad

12

ACROSS

1 Smart __ whip
4 "No __, ands, or buts!"
7 Polite term of address
12 1400, in Roman numerals
13 Feel sorry about
14 Wear away
15 Pennsylvania site of Merion
17 Fit for a king
18 Beauty parlor
19 1999 Bob Hope champ
21 Risky business, for short
22 Monogram of Eisenhower's '56 opponent
23 __ Pak of the LPGA
26 Souped-up auto
29 Former Byron Nelson Classic sponsor
30 Prepare leftovers
33 Ship officer
35 From __ Z
36 Home of Jamie Farr's LPGA tourney
38 Sergeants, for example: Abbr.
40 Tiger, to Earl
41 Talking horse of TV
45 Chips and drives
47 Mr. Stewart
48 Lord's home
50 Lightning partner
52 General Bradley's namesakes
53 Two-year-old
54 Botch
55 "We __ please!"
56 Fall month: Abbr.
57 Cowboy hero Rogers

DOWN

1 Pile up
2 Throw out
3 Confuse
4 Approach club
5 Mink or sable
6 Lawn tool
7 Griffin of game shows
8 Vicinities
9 Holes with a bend

10 Dentists' organization: Abbr.

11 Actor Gibson

16 Coffee/chocolate combo

20 One of the majors

22 Maximally

24 Highway: Abbr.

25 Comparative suffix

27 Dinner-table morsel

28 Fizzler

30 Rolled after landing

31 And so on: Abbr.

32 1991 Masters champ

34 Caesar or Antony

37 Was defeated by

39 Not quite on the green

42 Doral-__ Open

43 First month, in Mexico

44 County of Ireland

46 Approximately

47 Hole out

48 Extinct bird

49 Friend, in France

51 Ad __ committee

13

ACROSS

1 Caddie's burden
4 Hole-in-one prize, at times
7 Fortune-teller of India
12 Mobile's state: Abbr.
13 Pub offering
14 Des Moines native
15 Remote
16 Was in first place
17 Attendees
18 Climactic time of a tourney
21 Miss the __
22 Golf bet
26 Tropical spots
29 British Open month: Abbr.
30 Keyboard key
31 Hit the ball
32 Beast of the zodiac
33 One of Trevino's gallery
34 J.C.'s uncle
35 Mr. January
36 Best ball, for example
37 1998 Masters champ
39 Feel under the weather
40 1974 British Open champ
45 Norman's nickname
48 One of the Oceans: Abbr.
49 Yoko __
50 Eagle on a par five
51 Golfer Elder
52 Abbreviation on a scorecard
53 __ away from (avoids)
54 Mess up
55 World War II spy group: Abbr.

DOWN

1 Hit a golf ball badly
2 Jai __
3 Former senator Jake
4 Golfer's annoyance
5 At the ready
6 Make over
7 Flare or lighthouse
8 1997 Masters champ

9 Overwhelm
10 Damage
11 Elected officials
19 __-deucey
20 *E pluribus* __
23 Table condiment
24 Actor Guinness
25 Provo's state
26 __ facto
27 Grand __

28 Like some excuses
29 Ms. Stephenson
32 Lion's sound
33 '40s White House dog
35 Male ducks
36 1976 British Open champ
38 See eye to eye
39 More quick to learn

41 New Haven university
42 Toy on a string
43 Concludes
44 Seamstress Betsy
45 Thoroughfares: Abbr.
46 Initials of LBJ's vice president
47 *Exodus* hero

ACROSS

1 Billiards equipment
5 Golfer's target
9 They cross avenues: Abbr.
12 Prefix meaning "against"
13 What "+" means on a leader board
14 Golf teacher, often
15 1994 British Open champ
17 Snakelike fish
18 Color
19 Game-show host
21 Brag
24 Mr. Crosby
26 Inept one
27 Sci-fi vehicles: Abbr.
29 State of mind
33 Lema's nickname
36 Subjective atmosphere
37 Allows
38 Last letter
39 1991 PGA Championship winner
41 Winner of 81 PGA tournaments
43 __ spot
46 Where each hole starts
47 Hush-hush organization: Abbr.
48 Golf-lesson subject
54 Canadian province: Abbr.
55 Slangy suffix
56 Adam and Eve's home
57 Quarterback stat: Abbr.
58 Short putts
59 Letters on an invitation

DOWN

1 Soup holder
2 Prefix meaning "one"
3 List-shortening abbreviation
4 Muslim sect
5 Fairway shout
6 XXVIII doubled
7 Nuclear Regulatory Commission predecessor: Abbr.
8 1985 PGA Championship winner
9 On __ (riskily)
10 Out-of-bounds hazard
11 Golf-club part

16 Post, as a leaderboard score
20 Group in charge: Abbr.
21 __ Raton, Fla.
22 Honolulu's island
23 From a distance
24 Good score for a duffer
25 Does not exist
28 Drop down in the standings

30 Seep slowly
31 Highly rated
32 Changed the color of
34 Manufactured
35 Road curves
40 Facing the pitcher
42 More recent
43 Paul Lawrie, e.g.
44 Ball-carrying factor
45 Snacks on

46 Boxing results
49 Coach Parseghian
50 Joe Friday, for one
51 Airport-security concerns: Abbr.
52 PageNet Championship locale: Abbr.
53 Economic stat: Abbr.

15

ACROSS

1 Ewe's baby
5 Cooling-system outlet
9 Sea plea
12 Margarine
13 Director Kazan
14 Recipe phrase
15 Something to shoot at
17 Singer Tormé
18 Actress Liv
19 Locksmith's creations
21 Golf-course distance unit
24 2000 Masters winner
27 Tiny pencil
30 __ and turf
32 Brazilian soccer great
33 Norwegian name
35 __ *Abner*
36 Author Bellow
37 Something inside an envelope: Abbr.
38 Like Darth Vader
40 Rep.'s rival
41 Fairway hazards, at times
43 Fencing blade
45 When the Ryder Cup was held in 1999: Abbr.
47 Heavenly being
51 Edge of a cup
53 Nicklaus' alma mater
56 Numerical prefix
57 Golf-course hospitality structure
58 Sandberg of baseball
59 __ Francisco
60 Transmitted
61 Rookie of the __

DOWN

1 What a wedge provides
2 Comrade
3 Brunch, for instance
4 Fail to save par
5 American Legion member
6 Actor Wallach
7 Mr. Faldo
8 __ first (wins)

9 Oldest player to win a PGA event

10 Grand __ Opry

11 Actor Mineo

16 Spanish women: Abbr.

20 9 Down's putting woe

22 Penalty reason

23 First shot

25 Stick together

26 Ship captain's place

27 Christmas season

28 Forearm bone

29 Why a shot may stop abruptly

31 Upend

34 Escape

39 Meadows

42 Places in a tournament field

44 Access

46 "Of __ I Sing"

48 Soul singer Marvin

49 Sicilian volcano

50 Impolite look

51 Recent West Point grads: Abbr.

52 Author Levin

54 Quaint hotel

55 Baseball great Mel

16

ACROSS

1 Shine brightly
5 Just published
8 Attention-getting sound
12 Singing syllables
13 Dictator Amin
14 AAA suggestions: Abbr.
15 Actor Sharif
16 Greek letters
17 Pig's remark
18 1989 PGA Championship winner
21 First woman
22 Mr. Herron
23 When final rounds of tournaments are played

26 Discounted
30 Mao __-tung
31 Quarterback Dawson
32 Part of a golf club
36 Shade trees
39 Compass point: Abbr.
40 Davis Love __
41 Place to practice
47 Dangerous reptile
48 Family member
49 Well-ordered
50 Chess piece
51 Birdie on a short hole
52 Leave out
53 Makes a choice

54 Transgression
55 Only

DOWN

1 Unappetizing food
2 The Dalai __
3 Oil of __
4 Shouted "Fore!"
5 Comedian __ Russell
6 Do a newspaper job
7 Not fooled by
8 Types of tournaments
9 Agitate
10 Mailed away
11 Reproachful sound

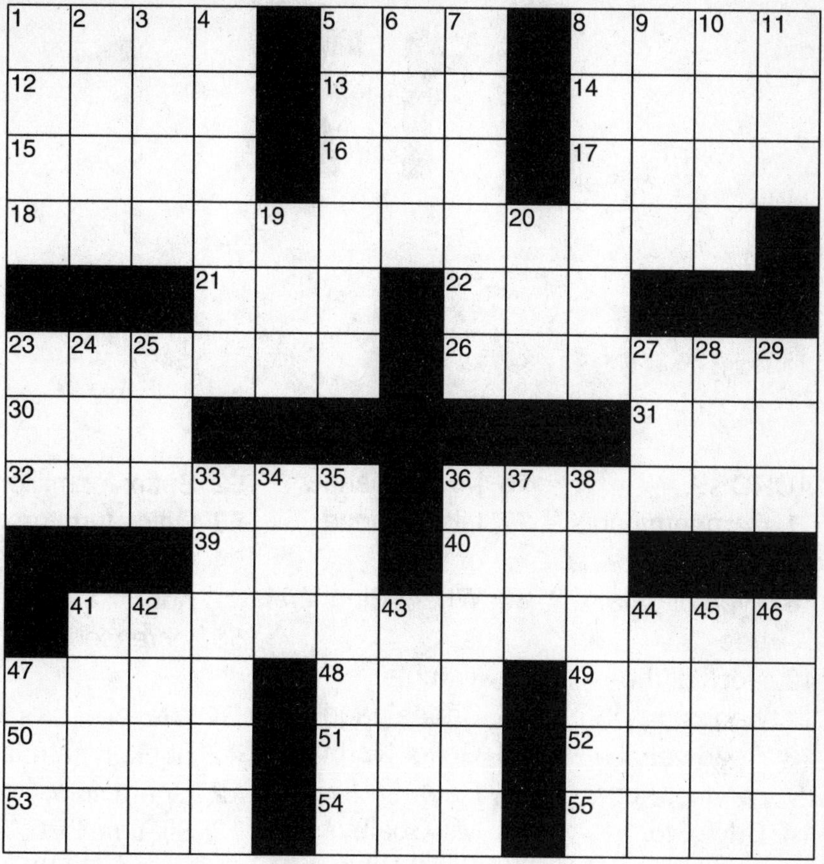

19 Zsa Zsa's sister
20 Take home the trophy
23 Lines on a map: Abbr.
24 Soldier hangout: Abbr.
25 __ Invitational (Tiger win in '99)
27 Everyone
28 Mr. Janzen
29 Naval officer: Abbr.
33 NBA team
34 Letter holder: Abbr.
35 Emulates Chubby Checker
36 Filet __
37 Put on television
38 Musical instruments
41 It may be free on a course
42 Encourage the team
43 "__ lay me down to sleep"
44 Jules Verne captain
45 Author Sheehy
46 Diminutive suffix
47 __-Magnon man

17

ACROSS

1 Carpentry tools
5 __ Miniver
8 Type of palm tree
12 Neck of the woods
13 Road-service service: Abbr.
14 Driver, for example
15 Nine irons
17 Concerning
18 Bit of hair cream
19 Course designer Pete
20 They may be knocked while putting
21 Distress signal
22 Tee, essentially
23 College-golf regulator: Abbr.
26 Mr. Crenshaw
27 Like a round of 170
30 Where Pinehurst is
34 Trouble
35 Canoe paddle
36 Golfer North
37 Dad
38 Mr. Goalby
40 Great White __ (Greg Norman)
43 Gold, in Mexico
44 Possesses
47 Georgetown athlete
48 He shot a 59 in Las Vegas in '91
50 Greater Hartford __
51 Industrious insect
52 Suffix for million
53 Office furniture
54 Golf-ball buy: Abbr.
55 Increased

DOWN

1 Bunker material
2 Opera solo
3 Six-time LPGA winner in '99
4 Bando of baseball
5 Thanksgiving Day parade sponsor
6 Bunker smoother
7 __ in "Snead"
8 Something to practice
9 First-rate
10 Clinton's vice president

11 Types of poems
16 Bachelor's last words
20 Gambling game
21 Took a load off
22 __ diem worker
23 Compass direction: Abbr.
24 Pigeon sound
25 Live and breathe
26 The 19th hole
27 Storage container
28 In addition
29 Golfer Glen
31 Errant drive
32 Golfer's headwear
33 Chem room
37 Practical joke
38 1979 U.S. Women's Open champ
39 "Alley __!"
40 Did a blacksmith's job
41 Desert Classic VIP
42 Affirmative votes
43 "This can't be!"
44 Inheritor
45 Farmland unit
46 Distort
48 No gentleman
49 Club holder

18

ACROSS

1 Greater Milwaukee Open locale: Abbr.
5 Old Testament book: Abbr.
9 Cry of discovery
12 Cube inventor Rubik
13 Tropical nut
14 Like greens after a storm
15 Boyfriend
16 Fairway selection
17 Cereal grain
18 Baltusrol's New Jersey locale
21 Give in to gravity
22 British Open beverage
23 Masters champs' jacket color
26 Like some shots
30 Feel under the weather
31 Was in first place
32 Golf-club parts
35 Works hard
37 Morse-code message
39 Clumsy one
40 1996 Players Championship winner
45 Reason for sudden death
46 Long-hitting Senior pro
47 Matures
49 December 24th, for one
50 Noun suffix
51 *Rikki-Tikki-__*
52 Electrified fish
53 Moose relative
54 Genesis locale

DOWN

1 Spider's creation
2 Makes angry
3 Something simple
4 Colonial or Carnoustie
5 Approving
6 Bjorn of tennis
7 Where chip shots should go
8 1999 LPGA Hall of Fame inductee

9 Soldier's offense: Abbr.

10 Where the club hits the ball

11 Lawyer: Abbr.

19 Mr. Woosnam

20 __ de Cologne

23 Neon or oxygen

24 __ Grande

25 Letter after kay

27 151, in Roman numerals

28 Mr. Nagle

29 7,102, for Riviera: Abbr.

33 Language suffix

34 Installed a green

35 Gimme, maybe

36 Recently

38 Part of a play

39 External

40 Par for a 500-yard hole

41 Fishing need

42 __ upon a time

43 Old-time exclamation

44 PGA nickname

45 Ball supporter

48 Sermon topic

19

ACROSS

1 Baseball-team boss: Abbr.
4 Imported auto
7 Top-___ finish
12 Keogh relative
13 Quaint stopover
14 Like Santa Claus
15 A golf ball has 336 of them
17 Fairway-maintenance need
18 Three wood
19 Teeny-___
21 St. Jude Classic state: Abbr.
22 Souvenir of a 41 Across
23 Toy on a string
26 Sleepy and Sneezy
29 Winning streak
30 Pencil part
33 Not at all loyal
35 Mr. Kite
36 Money, in Mexico
38 Men-only party
40 Big name in Internet service
41 Hawaiian party
45 Country singer Travis ___
47 Golf course
48 Putting concern
50 Burton of the LPGA
52 Remote planet
53 Sounds of contentment
54 South American country: Abbr.
55 Bucolic
56 Tiny circle
57 "The Raven" poet's monogram

DOWN

1 Center
2 Complaint
3 Silents actor Novarro
4 Drying oven
5 Suffix for hero
6 Response
7 Large book
8 Dark wood
9 Where the Westchester Country Club is

10 Mao __-tung
11 That woman
16 Water hazards
20 France's __ Tower
22 Cowboy's rope
24 Actor Brynner
25 Eagle on a par three
27 Married

28 What corporals call colonels
30 Little green men: Abbr.
31 Go bad
32 Pro-to-be, perhaps
34 Mr. Montgomerie
37 Mediocre
39 Actress Garbo
42 Extreme

43 Director Kurosawa
44 Expend
46 Admired one
47 Unenviable tournament position
48 When baseball season starts: Abbr.
49 Prefix for perfect
51 Greek letter

20

ACROSS

1 Ken Venturi's network
4 Letters on a sunblock bottle
7 Three-time U.S. Women's Open champ
12 NASA affirmative
13 Baseball great Gehrig
14 Golf pro's asset
15 __ Classic (Hilton Head tourney)
16 Antique
17 Plane-tracking device
18 High-lofted clubs
21 It means "under par" on leader boards
22 Evaluation
26 One of a Nicklaus 20
29 Temporary craze
30 Hot drink
31 Golf pro's lesson
32 Mr. Colbert
33 When Hogan won his second U.S. Open
34 Tractor-trailer
35 Put on, as clothes
36 Western lake
37 Talks back to
39 For each
40 1984 PGA Championship winner
45 Jeans material
48 French assent
49 Clergy member: Abbr.
50 __ in Wonderland
51 Newhart setting
52 Silver source
53 Two-limbed creature
54 Table part
55 Neither's partner

DOWN

1 Machine parts
2 __ Raton, Fla.
3 Hole winner's prize, at times
4 Not as rapid
5 Propelled a gondola
6 Bugs Bunny's pursuer
7 Jam or jelly

8 Breakfast order

9 Assist

10 Civil War side: Abbr.

11 "__ out!"

19 Bit of rain

20 Metric weight

23 Hankering

24 Captain of the *Nautilus*

25 High wind

26 Bosses: Abbr.

27 Soprano's performance

28 Irish dances

29 Shark's visible part

32 __ Maria Cañizares

33 Sportscaster __ Albert

35 Considered

36 Preparing to drive

38 Duffer's drive, often

39 Dried fruit

41 Work too hard

42 Approach-shot club

43 Infamous Roman emperor

44 More than

45 Small quantity

46 Inventor Whitney

47 Small bite

21

ACROSS

1 Shot from the fringe
5 Portions of corn
9 Vanish into thin __
12 Number of PGA Championship titles won by Arnie
13 Club-face angle
14 Distance runner Sebastian
15 1996 Masters champ
17 Female sheep
18 Lubricate
19 __ play
21 Great golfer of the 1920s
24 Award from ESPN
26 Aussie bird
27 Right-hand man
29 Draw on glass
33 Famous course in Lancashire, England
36 Approximately
37 Data
38 Mongrel
39 Zilch, in Spanish
41 Aquatic mammal
43 Golf-bag attachment
46 The wild blue yonder
47 Hawaiian instrument
48 1995 LPGA Hall of Fame inductee
54 Barbecue bit
55 Curriculum division
56 Lake Ontario neighbor
57 Match Play Championship month: Abbr.
58 Department-store department
59 Auction, for example

DOWN

1 One of Ted Turner's networks
2 __ polloi
3 Letters on a business letterhead
4 Type of tea
5 Israeli airline
6 CompuServe alternative
7 Farm-mail abbr.
8 Jazzy dance
9 Sank a tee shot
10 Midwest state

11 Stagger
16 __ round (Sunday's tournament play)
20 Examined
21 Protagonist
22 Love, in Latin
23 PGA members
24 Minneapolis suburb
25 Feudal worker
28 Footnote abbreviation
30 Diplomacy
31 Detective's find
32 Mister, in Germany
34 First-rate
35 Peculiar
40 Photo book
42 Little kids
43 Gang's territory
44 "__ From Muskogee"
45 Million-dollar LPGA winner in 2000
46 Very fast planes: Abbr.
49 Compass point: Abbr.
50 Can metal
51 Lyricist Gershwin
52 Nothing
53 "That's amazing!"

22

ACROSS

1 Stow away
5 *Li'l Abner* cartoonist
9 Car drivers' organization: Abbr.
12 Jacob's Biblical twin
13 Singer Guthrie
14 Stay __ (don't move)
15 Biannual amateur event
17 One of the majors
18 Don't cry over __ milk
19 Plaintiff
21 Performs on stage
24 Investigate
27 Additionally
30 Sound of laughter
32 Shopping center
33 Beat decisively
35 Sea, in France
36 Sandra Haynie has had three of them
37 St. Louis landmark
38 Gymnast Korbut
40 Color
41 Ian __-Finch
43 The __ Ness Monster
45 Pressure, so to speak
47 __ Classic (March PGA event)
51 Sci-fi vehicle: Abbr.
53 1950s LPGA star
56 __ Paulo, Brazil
57 Wedge, for one
58 Scottish hillside
59 Seek to know
60 Pub projectile
61 Seeds a field

DOWN

1 Church seating
2 Right away, in memos
3 City in Colombia
4 __, *Fran and Ollie*
5 Hole-in-one prize, at times
6 Tee shot's path
7 Sign that means "over par"
8 Make an easy out, in baseball
9 Short shot to the green
10 Du Maurier Classic month: Abbr.

11 One __ time (individually)
16 Engrave deeply
20 Author Bombeck
22 __'-shanter (Scottish cap)
23 One-time *Wonderful World of Golf* sponsor
25 __ cheese dressing
26 Otherwise
27 Middle Easterner
28 Director Ephron
29 Duffer's drive, often
31 Jason's ship, in mythology
34 Quaker's pronoun
39 Feeling sore
42 Very quick
44 Redford's role in *The Natural*
46 *Gone With the Wind* mansion
48 Fictional sleuth __ Wolfe
49 Fade's opposite
50 Very long time
51 Walker Cup side
52 Notes of the scale
54 Rocky peak
55 Explosive initials

23

ACROSS

1 TV newsman Roger
5 Garden tool
8 See 40 Across
12 Biblical birthright seller
13 Masters month: Abbr.
14 Nautical command
15 Week-ending shout
16 Last letter
17 Camper's shelter
18 City near Pebble Beach
21 Ryder Cup side: Abbr.
22 Duo
23 Shot, for a round
26 Type of poem
30 Promissory note

31 Actress Gardner
32 Prepares to hit the ball
36 Winner of 51 PGA events
39 __ of bounds
40 With 8 Across, 1959 Masters champ
41 1947 Vardon Trophy winner
47 Subtle atmosphere
48 Pas' partners
49 Jules Verne captain
50 Happy
51 Call __ career (retire)
52 Biblical son
53 Sardine holders

54 Jug handle
55 Paramedics: Abbr.

DOWN

1 Shea Stadium team
2 Rules of Golf organization: Abbr.
3 *The __ Curse* (Hammett novel)
4 Not-so-great golfer
5 Bunker or lake
6 Ameritech Senior __
7 Builds
8 Senior Tour newcomer in 1999
9 Actor Baldwin

1	2	3	4	■	5	6	7	■	8	9	10	11
12				■	13			■	14			
15				■	16			■	17			
18				19				20				■
■			21				22					
23	24	25				26			27	28	29
30									31		
32			33	34	35		36	37	38		
■			39				40				■
■	41	42				43			44	45	46
47			■	48		■	49				
50			■	51		■	52				
53			■	54		■	55				

10 Letterman rival
11 Allow
19 Feel bad about
20 __ Jima
23 Family member
24 Dairy animal
25 Yes, in France
27 Snort snooze
28 Mother of 52 Across
29 Roofing material
33 Wanderers
34 Something to chew
35 Blocked putting situation of yore
36 Ancient Roman dictator
37 Club controller
38 Golfer's position
41 Ms. Inkster
42 Mideast nation
43 Numerical information
44 Package of paper
45 Give off
46 Large quantity
47 Player's representative: Abbr.

ACROSS

1 Taj Mahal's city
5 Kids' game
8 Walk tiredly
12 Part of the eye
13 Baseball stat: Abbr.
14 After-bath wear
15 Woods' playing partner in Round 1 of the 2000 PGA
17 Get __ the ground floor
18 Toll road: Abbr.
19 Make a choice
20 Three-putt result, maybe
21 Diamond weights: Abbr.
22 72, at Cypress Point
23 Mr. Olazábal
26 Busy month for greenskeepers: Abbr.
27 Opponent
30 Reason to pick up a ball
34 Pig's home
35 Country singer __ Clark
36 Five-time European Ryder Cup team member
37 Fort Worth school: Abbr.
38 Farm animal
40 1968 PGA Championship winner
43 __ good deed daily
44 Clean-air agency: Abbr.
47 Word of regret
48 Buick Open's state
50 1990 Buick Open champ
51 Pen filler
52 Word of warning
53 Senior golfer from Japan
54 Plaything
55 Words of understanding

DOWN

1 "__ We Got Fun?"
2 How a club is held
3 *Casablanca* character
4 Pose a question
5 Green guardians
6 Be next to
7 Draftees: Abbr.
8 Previous

9 Furthest off the tee

10 Bassoon relative

11 Declare untrue

16 Real-estate parcel

20 Best-__ tournament

21 Golfer Nagle

22 British tavern

23 Roast beef au __

24 2000 Canadian Open locale: Abbr.

25 Secret agent

26 Haas of the PGA

27 Go by air

28 Neat's-foot __

29 Wide shoe

31 Curved lines

32 "It Had to Be __"

33 Shade tree

37 Golf teacher to the pros Bob

38 Senior golfer Thompson

39 Ooh and __

40 Ali __

41 Margarine

42 Billiards accessory

43 Flintstones' pet

44 Swelled heads

45 Glass sheet

46 Poker ritual

48 Harvard neighbor: Abbr.

49 Dictator Amin

25

ACROSS

1 Flat boat
5 Animal-protection organization: Abbr.
9 Encountered
12 Gymnast Korbut
13 Star of *Arli$$*
14 __ *Got a Secret*
15 Pub projectile
16 Olympic skater Heiden
17 Letter after wye
18 July PGA event
21 Not at home
22 Had a snack
23 Tilted to one side
26 Eldrick's nickname
30 Feedbag morsel
31 Golf-loving president
32 Fairway material
35 __ out (finished putting)
37 "__ Not for Me to Say"
39 The First State: Abbr.
40 A PGA trophy is named for him
45 Jazz great Beiderbecke
46 Vocal
47 Ski lift
49 Feeling poorly
50 1997 Ryder Cup captain
51 "Excuse me!"
52 Cheer for a bullfighter
53 Simple
54 Veal or venison

DOWN

1 Greens material
2 Eagle's gripper
3 Meanie of folklore
4 1982 U.S. Open champ
5 Sugary
6 Cat sound
7 Fine dinnerware
8 1999 LPGA Hall of Fame inductee
9 1987 Masters champ
10 Leader-board word

11 From __ to green

19 Boy King of Egypt

20 Architect I.M. __

23 Fireplace filler

24 Dumbo's wing

25 __ standstill

27 Mr. Morgan

28 __ out a living

29 Obviously embarrassed

33 British title

34 Scoring unit

35 That woman

36 Morris Sr.'s nickname

38 Mideast nation

39 '60s Chicago mayor

40 Dave or Mike

41 Wheel shaft

42 Industrial tubs

43 Orchestral instrument

44 California wine valley

45 Palmer's *A Golfer's Life* is one

48 Alphabetic trio

ACROSS

1 Canonized people: Abbr.
4 Advice columnist Landers
7 1990 Masters champ
12 Big Internet service
13 Scare word
14 Designer Simpson
15 Longest-distance clubs
17 Stiff
18 Speed up: Abbr.
19 Eagle on a par five
21 At that time
22 Spanish woman: Abbr.
23 Army group

26 1998 British Open champ
29 Tumult
30 *The Wizard of Oz* character
33 Acts hospitably
35 Greek letter
36 __ Open (February PGA tourney)
38 Captures
40 Sounds of recognition
41 Korea's continent
45 Opening words
47 Religious images
48 High-tech medical tool
50 1977 PGA Championship winner
52 Banquet VIP
53 Blow up, as a photo: Abbr.

54 Author Deighton
55 1969 U.S. Open champ
56 Westchester Country Club's town
57 Commencement attendees: Abbr.

DOWN

1 Egyptian statesman
2 Olympics lighting
3 Errant drive
4 Cain's brother
5 "Neither rain __ sleet . . ."
6 Cosa __
7 Kroger Classic host
8 Parting words

9 Ben Hogan and Gene Sarazen
10 551, in old Rome
11 Multivolume dictionary: Abbr.
16 Cobra's weapon
20 Annoy
22 Competitor in The Tradition
24 Davis Love __

25 Country-music cable network
27 "That's one small step for a __ . . ."
28 Hungry __ bear
30 Midmorning
31 Call __ day (turn in)
32 Dinah Shore sponsor
34 Talent

37 It may interrupt a round
39 Senior pro Ed
42 Gets dirty
43 __ sanctum
44 Special-interest groups: Abbr.
46 Poker card
47 Not working
48 Lunar vehicle
49 I love, in Latin
51 Whichever

27

ACROSS

1 Some bank accounts: Abbr.
4 Ms. Mallon
7 LPGA Rookie of the Year in 1973
12 Authorize
13 Had a bite
14 "__ vincit amor" (love conquers all)
15 Actress Thurman
16 __ Na Na
17 British prisons
18 Left-handed Senior
21 Flagstick
22 Seafood serving
26 Reno-__ Open
29 "No __, ands, or buts"
30 NHL surface
31 Fusses
32 "Unforgettable" singer Cole
33 Taj Mahal town
34 Forty winks
35 __ Andreas fault
36 Match-play margin, at times
37 __ in regulation
39 Not in
40 Main reason for prize-purse increases
45 First Greek letter
48 Leg, slangily
49 Farm implement
50 Stuck in a swamp
51 Cheer for a matador
52 Light-switch positions
53 Megastars
54 Concordes: Abbr.
55 Bradley of the LPGA

DOWN

1 Wedge or wood
2 Floor model
3 Wild guess
4 Five iron
5 Vermont patriot __ Allen
6 Equipment
7 Pro's woes
8 Pile up
9 Numero __
10 Senior golfer Morgan

11 Possesses

19 Naval officers: Abbr.

20 Golf ball's height

23 Buster Brown's dog

24 Brown shade

25 Gather, as grain

26 Sharp taste

27 Hebrew month

28 Chrysler Classic host

29 Mr. Baker-Finch

32 One-time soccer league: Abbr.

33 Strong insects

35 J.C. and Sam

36 U.S. Amateur champ in 1914

38 Singer Merman

39 Ellipses

41 Swelled heads

42 Flapjack chain's initials

43 Mrs. Charlie Chaplin

44 Bird's home

45 "What a good boy __"

46 Jar top

47 Golf teacher, often

28

ACROSS

1 Fairway choice
5 Jazz improvisation
9 Initials of FDR's successor
12 Deep sleep
13 Sector
14 Sturdy tree
15 2000 British Open site
17 Long, long __
18 Neckwear
19 Ben Crenshaw's home
21 Repair a computer program
24 Very narrow shoe
26 Former name of Tokyo
27 Adherents: Suff.
29 Clinton attorney general
33 First woman to design golf courses
36 Run __ (rant)
37 Highlander
38 Mao __-tung
39 Composer Stravinsky
41 Flower holders
43 Ms. Caponi
46 __-tac-toe
47 __ de Janeiro
48 Akron course
54 Ancient
55 Chimney channel
56 West Coast state: Abbr.
57 Letter additions: Abbr.
58 __ out a living
59 Start over with

DOWN

1 Medicine dosage: Abbr.
2 Auction unit
3 Actress Thurman
4 African language
5 LPGA's scoring trophy
6 "All the Things You __"
7 Kitten's sound
8 Spaghetti, for example
9 Sham
10 Long story

11 Boxing wins:
   Abbr.
16 Finger or toe
20 Merit
21 __ vu
22 Dutch cheese
23 Lawyer's pro __
   work
24 Even, on the
   course
25 Tennis great
   Arthur

28 Type of lily
30 Guesses: Abbr.
31 Winning margin,
   at times
32 Change for
   a five
34 Onion covering
35 "Love Me
   Tender"
   singer
40 Mistake
42 Cast member

43 Just a __ in
   the bucket
44 Lubricates
45 Silent assents
46 Prepared to
   drive
49 Variety
50 Feel bad
   about
51 Metallic rock
52 Actor Beatty
53 Self-image

29

ACROSS

1 Assist in a crime
5 Pre-tournament posting
9 Wrestling surface
12 Actor Bridges
13 Owl sound
14 Thurman of *The Avengers*
15 1987 Ryder Cup team member
17 Strong cleaner
18 Mr. Els
19 Daredevil Knievel
21 Poet Odgen
24 Andrew Lloyd Webber musical
27 Bounce of a ball
30 Greet
32 Old-time exclamation
33 Coup d'__
35 Highway warning sign
36 Pro __ (proportionally)
37 Learning method
38 Counterfeit coin
40 Viet __
41 Back-to-health process, for short
43 Cease
45 Took advantage of
47 Kane of the LPGA
51 70, at Colonial
53 1992 British Open site
56 Geiberger's namesakes
57 Poker ritual
58 Space Shuttle organization: Abbr.
59 Do-it-yourselfer's buy
60 He caught Capone
61 British streetcar

DOWN

1 Well qualified
2 Yellowstone beast
3 Win on the Tour
4 City in Italy
5 Electrical unit
6 "Why __ Love You?"
7 Take a nap
8 Mr. Elkington
9 Free shot
10 Benz of the LPGA

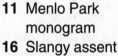

11 Menlo Park monogram

16 Slangy assent

20 At any time

22 Backtalk

23 Oakland ___ (Michigan course)

25 Parting words

26 Father of Abel

27 Mister, in Munich

28 Western Indian

29 1995 LPGA Rookie of the Year

31 Oaf

34 Pekoe and oolong

39 Game invented in Scotland

42 Former PGA Tour commissioner

44 Tiny circle

46 Sahara site

48 Bring up

49 *Casablanca* character

50 Dutch cheese

51 LPGA pro from Korea

52 Three-time heavyweight champ

54 Part of TGIF

55 Scale notes

30

ACROSS

1 Mr. Mickelson
5 401, to Caesar
8 __ along (follows)
12 Swiss river
13 Edge of a hole
14 USC rival
15 Horse-stopping word
16 Sixth sense: Abbr.
17 Highways: Abbr.
18 Winner of 42 LPGA events
21 Gobble up
22 Hawaiian garland
23 Senior pro Archer
26 Ms. Sörenstam
30 Author Fleming
31 __ Invitational (August PGA event)
32 Putting areas
36 Pre-shot motion
39 Watch the grandchildren
40 Compass point: Abbr.
41 Site of the 1996 U.S. Open
47 Stereo
48 Broken-down horse
49 Jack Nicklaus' son on the Tour
50 Grand __
51 Alphabetic trio
52 British prep school
53 Beginner
54 __ in "eagle"
55 Philosopher Descartes

DOWN

1 Cat's feet
2 Response to a joke
3 Wedge, for example
4 Pro at the top
5 Manufacture
6 Piece of dinnerware
7 African antelope
8 Call it a day
9 Start of a play
10 Happiness

11 Airline to Stockholm
19 Dustcloth
20 Japanese money
23 Musician's job
24 Rabbit feature
25 Washington's bill
27 Gerundial suffix
28 Golfer Nagle
29 Duffer's dream
33 Igloo builder
34 Zilch
35 Golf-lesson subject
36 Sand clubs
37 Hardwood tree
38 Physicist's __ counter
41 Like some paints
42 Worship from __
43 34 Down, in Spain
44 Past the deadline
45 Author Hubbard
46 "Auld Lang __"
47 Truman's monogram

31

ACROSS

1 Greek-salad ingredient
5 On a birdie-making streak
8 +
12 Retirement accounts: Abbr.
13 Have another birthday
14 Hard to hold
15 2000 PGA Championship site
17 Federal agent
18 Alaska native: Abbr.
19 "__ Got a Crush on You"
20 Mr. Beman
21 Eisenhower's monogram
22 Neither's partner
23 Mr. Couples
26 Wine and dine, perhaps
27 *Golf Digest* is one
30 1989 U.S. Open champ
34 Average grade
35 Like a rookie
36 Winged __ (New York course)
37 Chinese sauce source
38 The 19th hole
40 1995 U.S. Open champ
43 Litter member
44 Tiger Woods' home: Abbr.
47 Frequent forecast in 39 Down
48 Much of a course's real estate
50 California neighbor: Abbr.
51 And so on: Abbr.
52 Run __ (go bananas)
53 Ms. Daniel
54 "A mouse!"
55 Bears' homes

DOWN

1 Highest par on a hole
2 Historical periods
3 Converse
4 Fireplace residue
5 Tie a hole, in match play
6 Stare at
7 Hot drink
8 British golfer Oosterhuis
9 1964 British Open champ
10 __ Bator, Mongolia
11 "Auld Lang __"
16 Be of help to

1	2	3	4		5	6	7		8	9	10	11
12					13				14			
15				16					17			
18					19				20			
			21					22				
23	24	25				26				27	28	29
30				31	32				33			
34				35					36			
			37				38	39				
40	41	42				43				44	45	46
47					48				49			
50					51				52			
53					54				55			

20 Shut the __ (clinch a victory)
21 Banned insecticide: Abbr.
22 "I should say __!"
23 Television-regulating agency: Abbr.
24 Feel sorry for
25 Before, in poetry
26 Compass direction: Abbr.
27 Letters on a phone
28 In the past
29 Obtain
31 Approach-shot club
32 Utter
33 Congo's continent
37 2000 Masters champ
38 __ Open (August PGA event)
39 Spring month: Abbr.
40 In all likelihood: Abbr.
41 Swiss river
42 __ Nam
43 1976 U.S. Open champ
44 Hall of __
45 City in France
46 Pops the questions
48 Greens __
49 Thick bankroll

32

ACROSS

1 Breakfast side dish
5 One of the Simpsons
9 Nightclothes: Abbr.
12 Opera highlight
13 At any time
14 Drag around
15 __ pad (pond plant)
16 Interoffice note
17 Height: Abbr.
18 1969 U.S. Women's Open champ
21 Charged atom
22 Professor's degree: Abbr.
23 PGA pro Steve
26 Long time
30 "It's __-win situation!"
31 Notes of the scale
32 Physician
35 Par-five possibility
37 Gun owner's group: Abbr.
39 Gallery member
40 Bad place for a ball to be
45 Squid's weapon
46 Golf headliner
47 Bakery assistant
49 *Norma* __
50 Nick Faldo, for one
51 1990 U.S. Women's Open champ
52 Response: Abbr.
53 Ivy League school
54 Helps

DOWN

1 Mr. Sutton
2 Very dry
3 Farmer's storehouse
4 1974 LPGA Championship winner
5 Two-time U.S. Amateur champ
6 With, in France
7 Make a new chart of
8 Champ's prize
9 Make preparations
10 Ms. Inkster

11 G.I.'s superior: Abbr.

19 Numerical data: Abbr.

20 Poem of praise

23 Traffic tie-up

24 Indivisible

25 Get the __ (be selected)

27 De Vincenzo's homeland: Abbr.

28 Family member: Abbr.

29 Compass point: Abbr.

33 Bank-account posting: Abbr.

34 "Clambake" founder

35 __ de Cologne

36 Ms. Sörenstam

38 Performers' union: Abbr.

39 Specialty

40 __ even keel

41 Luau instruments

42 Judge's concern

43 CCCI doubled

44 Mail away

45 Author Levin

48 Football positions: Abbr.

33

ACROSS

1 Draft organization: Abbr.
4 Crankcase additive
7 En __ (together)
12 Hole played with no putts
13 *Ben-__*
14 Catchers' gloves
15 Arnold Palmer's hometown
17 Not at all polite
18 Untouchable Ness
19 Adored
21 Waiter's handout
22 Broadcast
23 Thick slice
26 1986 British Open champ
29 Recede
30 Competitor to beat
33 Military call
35 Get in, as a train: Abbr.
36 Golfer Gamez
38 Statistics
40 Mouthful of gum
41 Spheres
45 Important part of a golf swing
47 Make noise while asleep
48 Canizares' homeland
50 Finish putting
52 Looked at impolitely
53 Ecological agency: Abbr.
54 Ensign, for example: Abbr.
55 Come from behind
56 Mr. Floyd
57 Poetic nighttime

DOWN

1 Winston-__, North Carolina
2 Butcher's need
3 Become prevalent
4 Scored
5 Margarine holder
6 Main-event preceder
7 2105, to Nero
8 Buenos __
9 1982 Masters champ
10 Urban map lines: Abbr.
11 Superman's insignia

16 18 holes of golf
20 Gave a speech
22 Archery equipment
24 Defensive weapon: Abbr.
25 Air-gun ammo
27 "__ the fields we go . . ."
28 Oslo's country: Abbr.
30 Young fellow
31 Pitcher's stat: Abbr.
32 1959 PGA Player of the Year
34 Make amends
37 Beach patron
39 Shakespearean sprite
42 TV executive Arledge
43 Mr. Crampton
44 First American saint
46 __ 500 (annual auto race)
47 Do in
48 College club for women: Abbr.
49 One of Woods' 2000 championships
51 __-Locka, Fla.

34

ACROSS

1 Physique, for short
4 Peg for Palmer
7 252, in old Rome
12 Actor Wallach
13 Peanut product
14 In the lead
15 Aunt, in Mexico
16 Golfer Elder
17 Gives autographs
18 Biennual women golfers' event
21 Hubbub
22 Niblick alternative
26 Course designer George
29 Elected official, for short
30 Actress __ Marie Saint
31 Unique individual
32 __ Diego, Calif.
33 Nest-egg accounts: Abbr.
34 Substance in cells: Abbr.
35 Elevator compartment
36 In __ (leading)
37 Fountain of Youth searcher
39 One on Tour
40 First LPGA player with a $100,000 year
45 PGA pro O'Malley
48 Poetic nighttime
49 Solemn oath
50 Guinness and namesakes
51 August PGA event sponsor
52 Outer end of a clubhead
53 List of candidates
54 __-Cone (summer cooler)
55 2000 winner of The International

DOWN

1 Nassaus, for example
2 Miscellany
3 Dashboard device
4 Home of Jamie Farr's tournament
5 "Old MacDonald had a farm, __"
6 Grade school: Abbr.
7 Not at all formal
8 Short shots to the green
9 Tripod part
10 Mr. Woosnam

11 Driver's licenses, for example: Abbr.

19 Frog __ (bunker-border grass)

20 "Let's go!"

23 One who saves the day

24 __ the Terrible

25 __ Lansing (Oldsmobile Classic locale)

26 1957 Masters champ

27 Diarist Frank

28 Enthusiasm

29 71, at Baltusrol

32 Trap material

33 Household appliance

35 Robert Trent Jones design

36 2000 Compaq Classic champ

38 VCR button

39 Peacocks do it

41 Hankerings

42 1992 U.S. Open champ

43 Role model

44 Thumbs-down votes

45 Faux __ (minor mistake)

46 Right-angle shape

47 Boston __ Party

35

ACROSS

1 Pin
5 Bit of sunlight
9 Tallahassee school: Abbr.
12 Come up short in a playoff
13 Italian Renaissance painter
14 __ Lingus (Irish airline)
15 Greg Norman's homeland
17 B&O and Short Line: Abbr.
18 Where a hole starts
19 José __ Olazábal
21 Home of Firestone
24 Tiny branch
26 A wee hour
27 Matador's opponent
29 Oxidize, as iron

33 1991 British Open champ
36 Tower town in Italy
37 "Champagne Tony"
38 Mideast confederation: Abbr.
39 Tax-returns experts: Abbr.
41 Mr. Armour
43 Golf course
46 Battle of Britain participant: Abbr.
47 __ Dhabi
48 Famous course in Minnesota
54 Mr. Venturi
55 Greenspan of the Fed
56 Specialty of 55 Across: Abbr.

57 Visitors from space: Abbr.
58 Cried
59 Half of a course

DOWN

1 TPC at Sawgrass state: Abbr.
2 Comic Costello
3 Beast of burden
4 Reach
5 Hillside, at St. Andrews
6 Snakelike fish
7 "Gimme __!" (Start of an Indiana University cheer)
8 Terminus of U.S. 95
9 LPGA host Jamie
10 Pak of the LPGA
11 __ Minor (Little Dipper)

16 Designer Oscar de la __

20 Prefix for culture

21 "Take __ from me"

22 *The Bridge on the River* __

23 Director Howard et al.

24 Shot blockers, at times

25 Angler's bait

28 Texas neighbor: Abbr.

30 *E pluribus* __

31 Con game

32 Those folks

34 Prefix for spin or swing

35 __ *Attraction*

40 Old-time exclamation

42 All the time

43 Water hazard, perhaps

44 Remark of the skeptical

45 Parochial-school teachers

46 Monthly payment

49 Beer relative

50 Use the microwave

51 Here, in France

52 "Smoking or __?"

53 Compass direction: Abbr.

36

ACROSS

1 Type of pear
5 Shove
9 Auction activity
12 Opera solo
13 Slangy suffix
14 Historical period
15 1991 LPGA Championship winner
17 Scottish cap
18 Nixon's vice president
19 Snack
21 Designer Cassini
24 *Gone With the Wind* character
27 Car driver's document: Abbr.
30 Toboggan
32 Exxon's former name
33 Spot of land
35 Numero __
36 World War II turning point
37 Handle roughly
38 Late-night TV host
40 __ *gratia artis* (MGM motto)
41 Golfer Nichols
43 Wild guess
45 Listen to
47 1946 PGA Championship winner
51 Orange drink
53 Site of two Nicklaus U.S. Open wins
56 Type of snake
57 Small taste
58 Reebok rival
59 Conclusion
60 *M*A*S*H* star
61 Agitate

DOWN

1 Southern college, familiarly
2 Portland's state: Abbr.
3 Libra or Sagittarius
4 Walk-on role
5 Buddy
6 Internet address: Abbr.
7 Any day now
8 Right to tee off first
9 Congressional Golf Club locale
10 Lyricist Gershwin
11 Beaver's construction

16 Cobbler's tools

20 Tool building

22 Hebrew month

23 Sarazen et al.

25 Russian ruler of yore

26 Some Christmas presents

27 Arm or leg

28 With 49 Down, runner-up to Nicklaus in the 1980 U.S. Open

29 Ball striker

31 Word of warning

34 German river

39 Honolulu's island

42 "__ dabba doo!" (Fred Flintstone's cheer)

44 Naval officers

46 Horizontal bar

48 *True* __ (John Wayne film)

49 See 28 Down

50 Dodger or Astro

51 Lincoln's nickname

52 Put on, as clothes

54 Inc., in Britain

55 Chinese restaurant beverage

37

ACROSS

1 Winter weather
5 *Wide World of Sports* network
8 Of grand proportions
12 Entertainer Falana
13 Family member: Abbr.
14 Car
15 Take a crack __ (try)
16 One-time Chinese chairman
17 Mr. Norman
18 City near the Seniors' Vantage Championship
21 Nicklaus' alma mater: Abbr.
22 Poetic "before"
23 Amen __ (section of Augusta National)
26 Pete Dye's specialty
30 __ Francisco
31 Prefix meaning "new"
32 Ill-fated
36 Sand clubs
39 Mrs. Perón
40 Yoo or boo follower
41 1946 U.S. Open champ
47 Deceitful one
48 Four quarters: Abbr.
49 Folk knowledge
50 Three-time Vare Trophy winner
51 Female-name suffix
52 *Born Free* lioness
53 FedEx St. __ Classic
54 Portion of corn
55 Pleased

DOWN

1 Picnic side dish
2 Reply to the Little Red Hen
3 Actress Lena
4 First pro with a $500,000 year
5 "The Silver Scot"
6 1987 Ryder Cup team member
7 Like some stances
8 Duffers' impossible dreams

9 100%

10 Agenda component

11 Machine part

19 Literary monogram

20 Exist

23 Medinah clock setting: Abbr.

24 Canoer's need

25 Organic acid: Abbr.

27 Verbal suffix

28 Remark of the amazed

29 Thumbs-down votes

33 Golfer Bayer

34 Climbing plant

35 Fluff Cowan, for one

36 Vessel for Captain Ahab

37 Very long time

38 Fairway bend

41 In __ of (replacing)

42 Frying medium

43 "__ Lisa"

44 Move, as a ball on the green

45 Astronomical bear

46 Anthropologist Margaret

47 JFK's successor

ACROSS

1 Physicist's study
5 Truman's predecessor
8 Type of cereal
12 Stylish
13 Quarterback Dawson
14 Casino city
15 Pro whose real fist name is Theodore
17 Meal for a horse
18 Ha-ha relative
19 Biology or chemistry: Abbr.
20 Mr. Pavin
21 Seek to know
22 Antique
23 Low-quality
26 Greek letter
27 Club for car owners: Abbr.
30 37 Down buy
34 Use a sofa
35 Mover's vehicle
36 Golf organization headquartered in Daytona Beach: Abbr.
37 Color of the spectrum
38 Scale notes
40 Shingo Katayama's homeland
43 Jog
44 Flow back
47 Not invitational
48 Like some shorter golf courses
50 Sea-rescue agency: Abbr.
51 Ms. Alcott
52 Actor Sharif
53 Got up
54 "For shame!"
55 Pungent taste

DOWN

1 __-deucey
2 Finished, for short
3 Piglet's sound
4 April PGA tourney sponsor
5 1955 U.S. Open champ
6 Sandwich shop
7 Hospital professionals: Abbr.
8 Fowl family
9 Bring up
10 Penny-__ poker
11 Too inquisitive
16 Slalom curve

20 Country __
21 Noah's boat
22 Clumsy one
23 Commercial-free TV network: Abbr.
24 Yes, in Paris
25 Fall month: Abbr.
26 Heavy weight
27 High mountain

28 High-school math: Abbr.
29 Happy __ clam
31 At par
32 Tiny amount
33 Unser, Jr. and Sr.
37 Practice place
38 2000 Doral-Ryder Open champ
39 Aardvark snack
40 Soup du __

41 Lhasa __ dog
42 Chest muscles, slangily
43 St. Louis NFL team
44 Humorist Bombeck
45 Lima or pinto
46 Hazard to navigation
48 Ms. Bradley
49 On a __ streak

39

ACROSS
1 Shot in the dark
5 Air resistance
9 Except for
12 Killer whale
13 Accurate: Abbr.
14 Army officers: Abbr.
15 Henry VIII's last wife
16 Hint
17 Acorn producer
18 2000 U.S. Open site
21 Yale student
22 Response: Abbr.
23 Recreational game
26 Not quite on the green
30 Attention, so to speak
31 Poor grade
32 Real first name of "Walrus"
35 Mr. Elkington
37 Florida neighbor: Abbr.
39 Game-show prize
40 1969 LPGA Rookie of the Year
45 Urban transportation
46 In the neighborhood
47 Mr. Mickelson
49 Sort
50 Democratic-donkey creator
51 Golfer's goal
52 Army draftees: Abbr.
53 Quantities: Abbr.
54 Christmas season

DOWN
1 Soak (up)
2 One of 112 at the old Course at St. Andrews
3 Land measure
4 First Senior to reach $2 million in earnings
5 751, to Marc Antony
6 Acting job
7 Resort near Venezuela
8 __ fee (price to play)
9 Voting coalition

10 Novell ___ Showdown (Seniors event)
11 "A mouse!"
19 Sandwich order
20 Cookout residue
23 Minute fraction: Abbr.
24 72, at Winged Foot
25 "Are you a man ___ mouse?"
27 Keats poem
28 Gun the engine
29 Caddie's offering
33 Mr. Woosnam
34 LPGA great ___ Collett Vare
35 Actor Mineo
36 Presentation to a champ
38 Nautical direction
39 Course rentals
40 Ms. Inkster
41 Indulges one's curiosity
42 Be durable
43 ___ En-lai
44 Muffle, as sound
45 Immense
48 Mr. Janzen

40

ACROSS

1 Submissions to editors: Abbr.
4 College student's average: Abbr.
7 Golf-ball buy
12 Give __ go (try)
13 Hawaiian garland
14 Wear away
15 Thomas Bjorn's homeland
17 Cast off from the body
18 Three-time Masters champ
19 __ play (stroke play)
21 British conservative
22 Kometani of the LPGA
23 World Series preceder: Abbr.
26 It may be lucky on the course
29 Before, in poetry
30 Golfer Green
33 Real-estate account
35 Soldier show sponsor: Abbr.
36 Tampa neighbor
38 Small portions
40 Tee preceder
41 "Phooey!"
45 Golf journalist Longhurst
47 1971 U.S. Women's Amateur Champ
48 Hit a tee shot
50 Golfer Sifford
52 Super-__
53 *2001* computer
54 Pro from Johannesburg
55 Make changes to
56 Popeye's girlfriend
57 Be a spectator at

DOWN

1 Center
2 Office aide of the past
3 More sensible
4 Cheerful
5 __-diem worker
6 Pro quarterback Troy
7 Real-estate document
8 Ballpark instrument
9 1984 U.S. Open champ

10 Furgol's namesakes

11 After subtracting the handicap

16 Perhaps

20 Toastmasters

22 Texas wedge

24 __-Magnon man

25 Make a dress

27 Hospital areas: Abbr.

28 Clock setting at Augusta National: Abbr.

30 Paul Newman film

31 Ryder Cup side

32 Chrysler Classic host

34 Chest wood

37 Hitchcock thriller

39 Triple bogey on a par four

42 USGA concern

43 Spry

44 One of __ days

46 Egghead

47 Something to mark

48 Golf-loving president's initials

49 Jamaican drink

51 Horse feed

41

ACROSS

1 Boxing official
4 Home computers: Abbr.
7 Numbers on a calendar
12 Gold, in Mexico
13 Card game
14 Poetic Muse
15 Life story, for short
16 Vienna's country: Abbr.
17 Mr. Singh
18 Winner of 55 LPGA events
21 Complete collection
22 Actor Danny
26 PGA leading money winner in 1969
29 __ placement (important course factor)
30 Suffix for human
31 Stately trees
32 See the point of
33 Something taboo
34 Ball's position
35 One-liner
36 Golfer Alliss
37 1993 Masters champ
39 English tavern
40 1997 British Open site
45 Even
48 Gymnast's landing place
49 Byron Nelson Classic month
50 Performing
51 Geologist's suffix
52 Tax agency: Abbr.
53 Stockholm resident
54 Partner of neither
55 Mao __-tung

DOWN

1 LBJ in-law
2 Pennsylvania port
3 Short putt length
4 Went a round
5 Judge's workplace
6 Baseball slugger Sammy
7 Senior pro from Australia
8 Get up
9 __ Mahal
10 Greek letter
11 __ sauce (Chinese condiment)

19 Former Soviet Union components: Abbr.
20 Be patient
23 Ill-gotten gains
24 Bit of film dialogue
25 Aroma
26 Telephone inventor
27 Director Kazan
28 Prayer-ending word
29 Tee, essentially
32 Jack Nicklaus' golfing son
33 Omaha's st.
35 Course designer Fazio
36 Bobby Jones' "Calamity Jane"
38 __ slam
39 Greek philosopher
41 Dictator Idi
42 Leave out
43 Crew-team gear
44 NASDAQ rival: Abbr.
45 Commercials
46 Pull from behind
47 Fruit-filled dessert

42

ACROSS

1 Polite term of address

5 Senior pro Gibson

9 Defective bomb

12 Sheet of glass

13 Prefix meaning "against"

14 Military mailbox: Abbr.

15 JoAnne Carner's maiden name

17 Comic Costello

18 Suffix meaning "resident"

19 __ out a living

21 __-and-run shot

24 *Return of the __* (Star Wars film)

26 Numero __

27 Composer Stravinsky

29 Quipsters

33 Golfer honored on a U.S. postage stamp

36 Greek cheese

37 Three-piece suit part

38 Tempest __ teapot

39 Numbered highways: Abbr.

41 Less than

43 Mr. Mediate

46 Money player

47 Gold, to Ballesteros

48 1998 LPGA Player of the Year

54 Actor Gibson

55 Granny, for one

56 *"¿Cómo __ usted?"*

57 One of the majors

58 "Now it's clear!"

59 Calendar capacity

DOWN

1 Fuel-economy letters

2 Amateur-sports organization: Abbr.

3 Dear Abby's sister

4 Corpsman

5 Taxi cost

6 Hospital workers: Abbr.

7 World War I arena: Abbr.

8 Had a fine meal

9 Artist Salvador

10 "Once __ a time . . ."

11 Golfer Sanders

Across/Down	
16	Group of moral principles
20	New Zealand bird
21	Short blast of wind
22	Concerning
23	Precisely
24	Olazabal and namesakes
25	Greek love god
28	Donate
30	In the center of
31	Mr. Littler
32	Have the lead role
34	Antidrug officer
35	Road reversal
40	*The Touch System to Better Golf* author
42	Apt to pry
43	Frolic
44	West Coast state: Abbr.
45	Carbonated drink
46	Rose of baseball
49	Light-switch positions
50	Caviar
51	Poet Eliot's monogram
52	One __ time (individually)
53	Scratch the surface of

43

ACROSS

1 Place to play golf
5 Praise
9 Miss the __
12 Sociologist Shere
13 Canyon sound effect
14 *Norma* __
15 Tournament won three times by Tiger Woods
17 Hole-punching tool
18 Taj __
19 Soccer star Mia
21 Phrase of denial
24 1989 LPGA Hall of Fame inductee
27 Baseball arbiter
30 Makes a mistake
32 Diminutive suffix
33 Circus performer
35 Be obligated to
36 Rocky peaks
37 Actress Sorvino
38 Corporate subsidiaries: Abbr.
40 Fishing need
41 Mr. Stadler
43 11 P.M. broadcast
45 Chuck-wagon food
47 NEC Invitational locale
51 Air-conditioner unit: Abbr.
53 1994 British Open locale
56 Bering or Caribbean
57 *The Wizard of Oz* dog
58 Legalese phrase
59 Ms. Alcott
60 Roll-call count
61 19th-century political cartoonist

DOWN

1 Buddy
2 Walters of the LPGA
3 Salt Lake City's state
4 "Stadium golf" originator
5 Consent to
6 Poker card
7 Slangy refusal
8 Miami golf resort
9 Senior pro from Australia
10 Detroit union: Abbr.
11 __ Aviv

16 Succulent houseplant

20 Wine name

22 Walked on

23 1990 U.S. Open champ

25 Raison d'__

26 Gusto

27 Leathernecks' organization: Abbr.

28 Golda of Israel

29 Carlos Franco's homeland

31 Manuel Ballesteros' brother

34 Hideaway

39 Sailor's mop

42 __-percha

44 Flying geese

46 Harbor marker

48 Double-helix compound: Abbr.

49 Hockey great Bobby and family

50 Russian refusal

51 Merit-badge organization Abbr.

52 President pro __

54 AAA suggestion: Abbr.

55 Negative votes

44

ACROSS

1 Stadium level
5 __ for tat
8 Mr. O'Meara
12 *Goodbye, Columbus* author
13 One less than *dos*
14 Jai __
15 Furthest from the hole
16 One-quarter of M
17 Short comedic play
18 1983 LPGA Player of the Year
21 Medical-insurance company: Abbr.
22 "Why __ Love You?"
23 Shark Shootout host
26 Former House speaker Tip __
30 Sphere
31 Oxford and Cambridge Golfing Society home
32 LPGA great Mickey
36 Ties, in match play
39 Shelley poem
40 Three __ match
41 Three-time U.S. Senior Open winner
47 Like an 80-footer
48 Jack Nicklaus, to Gary
49 Nevada city
50 Short __
51 Actress Hagen
52 Course distance unit
53 Federal agent
54 Reimburse
55 Type of terrier

DOWN

1 Bunker
2 Council Bluffs' state
3 Coup d'__
4 "I Got __" (Gershwin tune)
5 February PGA stop
6 Fraction of a foot
7 July LPGA stop
8 One of the irons
9 __-Seltzer
10 Course drencher

11 Western scout Carson

19 Singer Sumac

20 Very long time

23 At this moment

24 NHL great Bobby

25 Baseball stat: Abbr.

27 Sportscaster Cross

28 Strong cleaner

29 Bandleader Brown

33 The __ Bear (Nicklaus)

34 The "good" cholesterol: Abbr.

35 Got ready to start a hole

36 Senior pro from South Africa

37 Santa __, Calif.

38 Mize's namesakes

41 Polite term of address

42 __ la Douce

43 Pro __ (proportionally)

44 Bird's bill

45 "Just You Wait, __ 'Iggins"

46 Took the train

47 Altitude: Abbr.

45

ACROSS

1 Mildred Didrikson's nickname
5 Tournament qualifying exemption
8 Metric-system prefix
12 Phrase of understanding
13 Golfer Hinkle
14 Jordanian
15 Mr. Langer
17 Highly objectionable
18 Drop
19 Propose
20 Group of tournament competitors
21 Quantity: Abbr.
22 Lifetime member of the European Tour
23 Driver
26 Type of snake
27 CD-__
30 Event played in non-Ryder Cup years
34 Month when spring starts: Abbr.
35 Operate
36 Botches the birdie
37 Steal
38 Tom Clancy group: Abbr.
40 __ Greater Hartford Open
43 "Gotcha!"
44 __ Perignon
47 Enjoy the course
48 Tiger Woods' college
50 "__ boy!"
51 Kultida, to Tiger
52 Feels regret
53 Window ledge
54 Balls-and-strikes caller
55 Stare at

DOWN

1 Babies' dinner wear
2 Making an ocean crossing
3 LPGA leading money winner in 1957
4 Poetic nighttime
5 Explosive shot
6 Pennsylvania city
7 Conclusion
8 Mr. Love
9 Buffalo's lake
10 Use the phone
11 Still sleeping
16 Deli meat
20 Not at all hilly
21 Source of magazine income
22 Very long time

23 Typist's speed: Abbr.

24 "Are you a man __ mouse?"

25 "__ the ramparts we watched . . ."

26 Mr. Crenshaw

27 Magnavox competitor

28 Yours and mine

29 Army cops: Abbr.

31 Household appliance

32 Name, as a knight

33 Fitness center

37 __ Melbourne (famous Australian course)

38 Trophy winner

39 Mr. Baker-Finch

40 Auditors' titles: Abbr.

41 Chorus members

42 Part of N.L.: Abbr.

43 Nuclear-power source

44 Mr. Sanders

45 Pitcher Hershiser

46 Retail inventory: Abbr.

48 Dallas school: Abbr.

49 To and __

46

ACROSS

1 "Stop, horse!"
5 Long story
9 Donkey relative
12 Diamond Head's locale
13 1965 PGA Championship winner
14 __ and aah
15 Not a duplicate: Abbr.
16 Composer Khachaturian
17 Point opposite SSW: Abbr.
18 Disastrous hole for a pro
21 Our sun's name
22 Bring legal action
23 LPGA great Berg
26 News-show summary
30 Lawyers' organization: Abbr.
31 Anger
32 1957 Vare Trophy winner
35 Mr. Hoch
37 Sing with closed mouth
39 __ la la
40 One of the majors
45 Moo goo __ pan
46 Spanish appetizer
47 Elevator inventor
49 Truck-regulating agency: Abbr.
50 Sign of the future
51 Something forbidden
52 Boxing result: Abbr.
53 Mr. Price
54 Look __ (visit)

DOWN

1 Wine and dine, perhaps
2 __ as nails
3 Memorial Tournament site
4 PGA Championship month
5 Tiny
6 Bern's river
7 Takes greedily
8 *How to Play Your Best Golf All the Time* author
9 Highest-rated
10 __ Open (January PGA event)

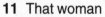

11 That woman

19 Tarzan's kid

20 "Golly!"

23 Mas' partners

24 __ Dhabi

25 Kids' game

27 AFL-__

28 Painting or sculpture

29 Poodle or parakeet

33 Letters on a phone

34 PGA leading money winner in 1983

35 Sign of Broadway success

36 1979 LPGA Championship winner

38 Florida city

39 Express one's appreciation

40 Support financially

41 Puerto __

42 Chancy enterprise, for short

43 British prep school

44 Baby boy, in Barcelona

45 "Vamoose!"

48 Family member

47

ACROSS

1 Mr. Wall
4 Business degree: Abbr.
7 Mistake
12 Pronoun for Miss Piggy
13 Unwell
14 Florida city
15 Home of the Masters
17 Type of pipe
18 Goblet parts
19 Winter Olympics competitor
21 Ms. Pak
22 __ out a living
23 Graceful bird
26 Home style
29 In the past
30 Green need
33 One of golf's "Big Three" in the '60s
35 Yoko
36 Unassuming
38 __ in the woods
40 Capek play about robots
41 Not of the clergy
45 Live and breathe
47 Mr. Lyle
48 After, in Paris
50 1984 LPGA Rookie of the Year
52 Prefix for violet
53 Before, to Keats
54 __ de Cologne
55 City in Japan
56 Carpentry tool
57 Draft agency: Abbr.

DOWN

1 Pile up
2 Traveling itinerary
3 Big name on the tour
4 Feel nostalgic for
5 Sandwich initials
6 Largest state
7 Asian desert
8 Course area units
9 Tee-to-green avenue
10 Home of 3 Down: Abbr.

11 Keep one's
___ to the
ground
16 Eskimo boat
20 ___ Open
(spring PGA
event)
22 Baseball
blunders
24 Mature
25 Neither's
partner

27 Not masculine:
Abbr.
28 1994 U.S. Open
champ
30 Unruly crowd
31 Santa ___,
Calif.
32 Mr. de
Vincenzo
34 Map book
37 Responsibilities
39 Bring to bear

42 Poker
payments
43 Notions
44 Reaper inventor
McCormick
46 Mr. Aoki
47 Distort
48 Arctic bird
49 Two-___
tissues
51 New Deal
agency: Abbr.

48

ACROSS

1 Letters on a speedometer
4 Misbehaving
7 Size of eggs
12 Abu Dhabi's confederation: Abbr.
13 Altar response
14 Less than
15 U-turn from NNW
16 Get free (of)
17 Puts on an agenda
18 Where Jamie Farr hosts an LPGA event
21 "__ is for her eyes, with love-light shining"
22 Mame, for one
26 1960 British Open champ
29 Cartoonist Capp's namesakes
30 Section of seats
31 Incoming planes: Abbr.
32 Reason for sudden death
33 Tiny amount
34 Notice
35 Dog's warning
36 Lee Trevino's home
37 Winner of two LPGA majors in 1974
39 __ Lanka
40 11 through 13 at Augusta National
45 AT&T Pebble Beach __
48 "Alley __!"
49 Author Levin
50 Pound fraction
51 Ordinal suffix
52 901, to Brutus
53 Chick sounds
54 Hog's home
55 Topeka's state: Abbr.

DOWN

1 Have to
2 El __, Texas
3 Clubhead part nearest the shaft
4 Par-beating hole
5 Lone Ranger's farewell
6 Extinct bird
7 __ Boros
8 Teamsters, for one
9 Physicians: Abbr.

10 Take the odds

11 Workplaces for 9 Down: Abbr.

19 Sushi-bar selections

20 Mr. Irwin

23 Kids' cereal

24 Tiny amount

25 Woolly beasts

26 Poet Ogden

27 Vicinity

28 Zane of westerns

29 Balloon filler

32 Magnolia or maple

33 Former Israeli prime minister

35 Very short putts

36 Vardon __

38 Civil-rights organization: Abbr.

39 Dunlap of the PGA

41 Negative votes

42 Mr. Faldo

43 Author Bombeck

44 One reason for a postponed round

45 Tiny explosion

46 Regret

47 Indivisible

49

ACROSS

1 Fly high
5 Author Ferber
9 Make an inquiry
12 Prefix meaning "against"
13 Takes a look at
14 Meadow
15 Ryder Cup format
17 Ms. Alcott
18 Door opener
19 Mr. Els
21 PGA Seniors' Championship month
24 1999 Ryder Cup team member
26 Cow's comment
27 Not of the clergy
29 It may be free on the course
33 Important part of a swing

36 French miss: Abbr.
37 Prefix meaning "outer"
38 __ Lanka
39 Openwork fabric
41 Angler's basket
43 Southern Hills Country Club locale
46 Hole in one
47 Exist
48 Senior Rookie of the Year in 1997
54 Major won four straight years by Hagen
55 Half of CXIV
56 Nevada neighbor

57 Member of Congress: Abbr.
58 Looked at
59 Shaquille O'__

DOWN

1 J.C.'s uncle
2 __ spree (reveling)
3 Lawyer: Abbr.
4 TV talk host Lake
5 Golf award given by ESPN
6 Pennsylvania neighbor: Abbr.
7 Teachers' union: Abbr.
8 So far
9 Actor Alda
10 Tractor-trailer truck
11 Actress Ballard

16 Word of welcome
20 Make over
21 Kind of radio
22 Motel amenity
23 Move on the green
24 Wedge shot
25 Eight, in Germany
28 Impresses mightily
30 Pretext

31 Mean one
32 Mr. Mickelson
34 Lunar vehicles
35 Mr. Mediate
40 Par-five possibility
42 Summer TV showing
43 Touches on the shoulder
44 Craving
45 Svelte
46 In the center of

49 College-wall climber
50 How the ball sits on the ground
51 __ Classic (February Seniors event)
52 Highly rated, as a bond
53 Stanley Cup awarder: Abbr.

50

ACROSS

1 __ d'oeuvres
5 Taxis
9 Baby goat
12 "Yipes!"
13 Worry
14 __ out a living
15 Neumann of the LPGA
17 Innovative
18 2000 Toshiba Senior Classic champ
19 Weight
21 Falsehoods
24 Place off the fairway
27 Letters on a sunblock bottle
30 Canadian Open month: Abbr.
32 Brown shade
33 Weirdo
35 Give, as odds
36 Variety-show act
37 Possessive pronoun
38 British nobles
40 Abbreviation on a scorecard
41 Gaffe
43 Golf-club part
45 Lasting impression
47 Barely ahead, in match play
51 What amateurs may turn
53 Winner of 88 LPGA events
56 Mr. Kite
57 Actress Anderson
58 All even
59 Fruit drink
60 Concordes: Abbr.
61 Legislative meeting: Abbr.

DOWN

1 __ on to (keep)
2 Kroger Senior Classic locale
3 Optimistic
4 __ Houston Open
5 Corporate bigwig: Abbr.
6 Creative skill
7 Ms. Daniel
8 Take the helm
9 Where Valhalla is
10 Eisenhower's nickname
11 Morning moisture in the fairway

16 Luau souvenirs
20 Enemies
22 Slippery fish
23 Where Bing Crosby played his last round of golf
25 Football field, for short
26 Crude houses
27 Type of terrier
28 Low-quality
29 Playing group
31 Robert __ Jones
34 Onetime McDonald's head
39 Garbage boat
42 Winner of eight LPGA majors
44 Nautical speed units
46 Greek letters
48 Toledo's lake
49 Western Indians
50 Graduate degrees: Abbr.
51 Public-school organization: Abbr.
52 Golfer Funseth
54 Bank-account posting: Abbr.
55 "__ the season to be jolly . . ."

ANSWERS

1

```
CABS   MOMS   BOB
ROUT   NOAH   ERE
AKRONOHIO     NAT
BILLY     MESH
    ESPY   SLOOP
BUB   EROO   EGGS
APER   OUR   WARS
JOSE   SNAP   NET
ANTES     GLEN
    BLUR   NOBLE
SEA   SEVENIRON
KEL   HAIR   SILO
ILL   IDEA   YEAS
```

2

```
CHET   FLA   STAG
LONE   REM   TENT
USGA   III   RENO
BERMUDAGRASS
    USA   OUI
FLOPSY   SENSOR
EEL          ALA
BEETLE   EMBODY
    RAN   MAY
  TRIPLEBOGEYS
CROC   AGO   OPIE
LEAK   COS   SEPT
VERY   ESS   HESS
```

3

```
FALA   AVA   LETS
AWOL   LAP   ALOE
DAVEMARR     USGA
EYE   CRY   AREAS
    TIM   MOA
ETCH   YAK   UFO
BABEDIDRIKSON
BUS   ELS   IAGO
    HAL   JAN
ROBED   PAR   AGE
ERIE   SUPERMEX
BALL   ERA   HERE
ALLS   TEN   ONES
```

4

```
GRAD   BRAD   CIA
NITE   ROLE   ARM
POND   ASAP   RAY
 TOURNAMENTS
     COD   ONE
CRIED       DODGE
NUN          ATA
NBCTV       ASSET
    EAR   SCH
  BALLESTEROS
LOS   LALA   EVEN
ELS   ERIC   WEVE
ATT   EMMY   DREW
```

5

```
CCS   TOE   TALIA
HAI   ERR   ERICS
ADDRESS     ANTES
IDEAS     ADMIT
RYAN   GTE   ELLA
    TARZAN   EER
TACOMA   ROARER
AIL   THUMBS
BRAG   ATE   COPE
    SLOMO   SOLID
HASON   PUTTING
DRIVE   ISA   VEE
LACES   ACT   ESS
```

6

```
SHE   SSS   WEDGE
LOP   POE   ARIAS
ICE   RUN   LADLE
THEMASTERS
    INA   SUEDES
SWING   VPS   ALA
HIRE   MAY   CLIII
ENE   SON   ROYAL
ADDSTO     NOW
  CARNOUSTIE
EATEN   INN   OFT
BLANC   NOD   USO
BETTE   ESS   RON
```

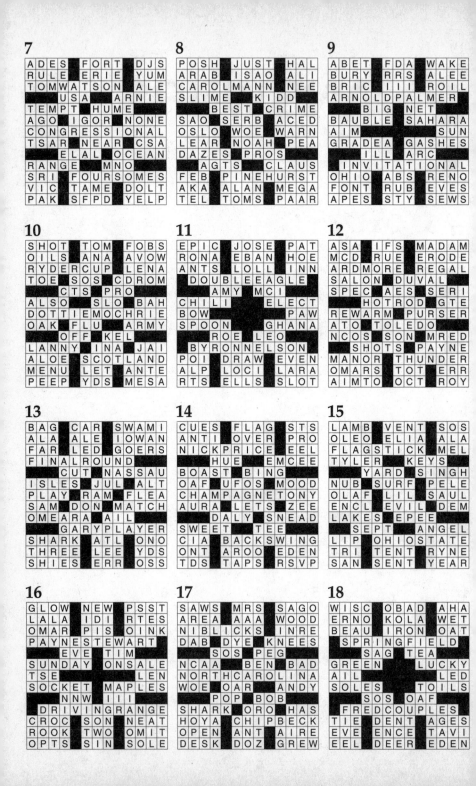

7

```
A D E S ■ F O R T ■ D J S
R U L E ■ E R I E ■ Y U M
T O M W A T S O N ■ A L E
■ ■ ■ U S A ■ ■ A R N I E
T E M P T ■ H U M E ■ ■ ■
A G O ■ I G O R ■ N O N E
C O N G R E S S I O N A L
T S A R ■ N E A R ■ C S A
■ ■ ■ E L A L ■ O C E A N
R A N G E ■ ■ M N O ■ ■ ■
S R I ■ F O U R S O M E S
V I C ■ T A M E ■ D O L T
P A K ■ S F P D ■ Y E L P
```

8

```
P O S H ■ J U S T ■ H A L
A R A B ■ I S A O ■ A L I
C A R O L M A N N ■ N E E
S L I M E ■ ■ K I D D ■ ■
■ ■ ■ B E S T ■ C R I M E
S A O ■ S E R B ■ A C E D
O S L O ■ W O E ■ W A R N
L E A R ■ N O A H ■ P E A
D A Z E S ■ P R O S ■ ■ ■
■ ■ A G T S ■ ■ C L A U S
F E B ■ P I N E H U R S T
A K A ■ A L A N ■ M E G A
T E L ■ T O M S ■ P A A R
```

9

```
A B E T ■ F D A ■ W A K E
B U R Y ■ R R S ■ A L E E
B R I C ■ I I I ■ R O I L
A R N O L D P A L M E R ■
■ ■ ■ B I G ■ ■ N E T ■ ■
B A U B L E ■ S A H A R A
A I M ■ ■ ■ ■ ■ ■ S U N
G R A D E A ■ G A S H E S
■ ■ I L L ■ ■ A R C ■ ■ ■
■ I N V I T A T I O N A L
O H I O ■ A B S ■ R E N O
F O N T ■ R U B ■ E V E S
A P E S ■ S T Y ■ S E W S
```

10

```
S H O T ■ T O M ■ F O B S
O I L S ■ A N A ■ A V O W
R Y D E R C U P ■ L E N A
T O E ■ S O S ■ C D R O M
■ ■ ■ C T S ■ P R O ■ ■ ■
A L S O ■ ■ S L O ■ B A H
D O T T I E M O C H R I E
O A K ■ F L U ■ A R M Y
■ ■ ■ O F F ■ K E L ■ ■ ■
L A N N Y ■ I N A ■ J A I
A L O E ■ S C O T L A N D
M E N U ■ L E T ■ A N T E
P E E P ■ Y D S ■ M E S A
```

11

```
E P I C ■ J O S E ■ P A T
R O N A ■ E B A N ■ H O E
A N T S ■ L O L L ■ I N N
■ D O U B L E E A G L E ■
■ ■ ■ A M Y ■ M C I ■ ■ ■
C H I L I ■ ■ E L E C T
B O W ■ ■ ■ ■ ■ ■ P A W
S P O O N ■ ■ G H A N A
■ ■ ■ R O E ■ L E O ■ ■ ■
■ B Y R O N N E L S O N ■
P O I ■ D R A W ■ E V E N
A L P ■ L O C I ■ L A R A
R T S ■ E L L S ■ S L O T
```

12

```
A S A ■ I F S ■ M A D A M
M C D ■ R U E ■ E R O D E
A R D M O R E ■ R E G A L
S A L O N ■ D U V A L ■ ■
S P E C ■ A E S ■ S E R I
■ ■ ■ H O T R O D ■ G T E
R E W A R M ■ P U R S E R
A T O ■ T O L E D O ■ ■ ■
N C O S ■ S O N ■ M R E D
■ ■ S H O T S ■ P A Y N E
M A N O R ■ T H U N D E R
O M A R S ■ T O T ■ E R R
A I M T O ■ O C T ■ R O Y
```

13

```
B A G ■ C A R ■ S W A M I
A L A ■ A L E ■ I O W A N
F A R ■ L E D ■ G O E R S
F I N A L R O U N D ■ ■ ■
■ ■ ■ C U T ■ N A S S A U
I S L E S ■ J U L ■ A L T
P L A Y ■ R A M ■ F L E A
S A M ■ D O N ■ M A T C H
O M E A R A ■ A I L ■ ■ ■
■ ■ ■ G A R Y P L A Y E R
S H A R K ■ A T L ■ O N O
T H R E E ■ L E E ■ Y D S
S H I E S ■ E R R ■ O S S
```

14

```
C U E S ■ F L A G ■ S T S
A N T I ■ O V E R ■ P R O
N I C K P R I C E ■ E E L
■ ■ ■ H U E ■ ■ E M C E E
B O A S T ■ B I N G ■ ■ ■
O A F ■ U F O S ■ M O O D
C H A M P A G N E T O N Y
A U R A ■ L E T S ■ Z E E
■ ■ ■ D A L Y ■ S N E A D
S W E E T ■ ■ T E E ■ ■ ■
C I A ■ B A C K S W I N G
O N T ■ A R O O ■ E D E N
T D S ■ T A P S ■ R S V P
```

15

```
L A M B ■ V E N T ■ S O S
O L E O ■ E L I A ■ A L A
F L A G S T I C K ■ M E L
T Y L E R ■ ■ K E Y S ■ ■
■ ■ ■ Y A R D ■ S I N G H
N U B ■ S U R F ■ P E L E
O L A F ■ L I L ■ S A U L
E N C L ■ E V I L ■ D E M
L A K E S ■ E P E E ■ ■ ■
■ ■ S E P T ■ ■ A N G E L
L I P ■ O H I O S T A T E
T R I ■ T E N T ■ R Y N E
S A N ■ S E N T ■ Y E A R
```

16

```
G L O W ■ N E W ■ P S S T
L A L A ■ I D I ■ R T E S
O M A R ■ P I S ■ O I N K
P A Y N E S T E W A R T ■
■ ■ ■ E V E ■ ■ T I M ■ ■
S U N D A Y ■ O N S A L E
T S E ■ ■ ■ ■ ■ ■ L E N
S O C K E T ■ M A P L E S
■ ■ N N W ■ ■ I I I ■ ■ ■
■ D R I V I N G R A N G E
C R O C ■ S O N ■ N E A T
R O O K ■ T W O ■ O M I T
O P T S ■ S I N ■ S O L E
```

17

```
S A W S ■ M R S ■ S A G O
A R E A ■ A A A ■ W O O D
N I B L I C K S ■ I N R E
D A B ■ D Y E ■ K N E E S
■ ■ ■ S O S ■ P E G ■ ■ ■
N C A A ■ ■ B E N ■ B A D
N O R T H C A R O L I N A
W O E ■ O A R ■ ■ A N D Y
■ ■ ■ P O P ■ B O B ■ ■ ■
S H A R K ■ O R O ■ H A S
H O Y A ■ C H I P B E C K
O P E N ■ A N T ■ A I R E
D E S K ■ D O Z ■ G R E W
```

18

```
W I S C ■ O B A D ■ A H A
E R N O ■ K O L A ■ W E T
B E A U ■ I R O N ■ O A T
■ S P R I N G F I E L D ■
■ ■ ■ S A G ■ ■ T E A ■ ■
G R E E N ■ ■ ■ L U C K Y
A I L ■ ■ ■ ■ ■ ■ L E D
S O L E S ■ ■ ■ T O I L S
■ ■ S O S ■ ■ O A F ■ ■ ■
■ F R E D C O U P L E S ■
T I E ■ D E N T ■ A G E S
E V E ■ E N C E ■ T A V I
E E L ■ D E E R ■ E D E N
```

19

```
MGR.KIA.TENTH
IRA.INN.OBESE
DIMPLES.MOWER
SPOON.WEENY..
TENN.LEI.YOYO
..DWARFS.RUN.
ERASER.FICKLE
TOM.DINERO...
STAG.AOL.LUAU
..TRITT.LINKS
SPEED.BRANDIE
PLUTO.AHS.URU
RURAL.DOT.EAP
```

20

```
CBS.SPF.STACY
AOK.LOU.POISE
MCI.OLD.RADAR
SANDWEDGES...
...RED.RATING
MAJOR.FAD.TEA
GRIP.JIM.MCML
RIG.DON.TAHOE
SASSES.PER...
.LEETREVINO..
DENIM.OUI.REV
ALICE.INN.ORE
BIPED.LEG.NOR
```

21

```
CHIP.EARS.AIR
NONE.LOFT.COE
NICKFALDO.EWE
...OIL.MEDAL.
HAGEN.ESPY...
EMU.AIDE.ETCH
ROYALBIRKDALE
ORSO.INFO.CUR
..NADA.OTTER.
TOWEL..SKY...
UKE.BETSYKING
RIB.UNIT.ERIE
FEB.MENS.SALE
```

22

```
PACK.CAPP.AAA
ESAU.ARLO.PUT
WALKERCUP.PGA
SPILT.SUER...
.ACTS.PROBE..
AND.HAHA.MALL
ROUT.MER.ACES
ARCH.OLGA.HUE
BAKER.LOCH...
.HEAT.HONDA..
UFO.PATTYBERG
SAO.IRON.BRAE
ASK.DART.SOWS
```

23

```
MUDD.HOE.WALL
ESAU.APR.ALEE
TGIF.ZEE.TENT
SANFRANCISCO.
..EUR.TWO....
SCORED.SONNET
IOU...AVA....
SWINGS.CASPER
.OUT.ART.....
JIMMYDEMARET.
AURA.MAS.NEMO
GLAD.ITA.CAIN
TINS.EAR.EMTS
```

24

```
AGRA.TAG.PLOD
IRIS.RBI.ROBE
NICKLAUS.INON
TPK.OPT.BOGEY
..KTS.PAR....
JOSE..JUL.FOE
UNPLAYABLELIE
STY.ROY.LYLE.
..TCU.RAM....
BOROS.DOA.EPA
ALAS.MICHIGAN
BECK.INK.DONT
AOKI.TOY.ISEE
```

25

```
SCOW.SPCA.MET
OLGA.WUHL.IVE
DART.ERIC.ZEE
.WESTERNOPEN.
.OUT.ATE.....
LEANT..TIGER.
OAT...IKE....
GRASS..HOLED.
.ITS.DEL.....
.HARRYVARDON.
BIX.ORAL.TBAR
ILL.KITE.OOPS
OLE.EASY.MEAT
```

26

```
STS.ANN.FALDO
AOL.BOO.ADELE
DRIVERS.RIGID
ACCEL.THREE..
THEN.SRA.UNIT
..OMEARA.DIN.
TINMAN.ASKSIN
ETA.NISSAN...
NABS.OHS.ASIA
.INTRO.ICONS.
LASER.WADKINS
EMCEE.ENL.LEN
MOODY.RYE.SRS
```

27

```
CDS.MEG.BAUGH
LET.ATE.OMNIA
UMA.SHA.GAOLS
BOBCHARLES...
..PIN.OYSTER.
TAHOE.IFS.ICE
ADOS.NAT.AGRA
NAP.SAN.ONEUP
GREENS.OUT...
.TELEVISION..
ALPHA.GAM.HOE
MIRED.OLE.ONS
IDOLS.SST.PAT
```

28

```
CLUB.VAMP.HST
COMA.AREA.OAK
STANDREWS.AGO
..TIE.TEXAS..
DEBUG.AAAA...
EDO.ISTS.RENO
JANSTEPHENSON
AMOK.GAEL.TSE
.IGOR.VASES..
DONNA.TIC....
RIO.FIRESTONE
OLD.FLUE.OREG
PSS.EKED.REDO
```

29

```
ABET.ODDS.MAT
BEAU.HOOT.UMA
LARRYMIZE.LYE
ERNIE.EVEL...
..NASH.EVITA.
HOP.HAIL.EGAD
ETAT.SLO.RATA
ROTE.SLUG.NAM
REHAB.STOP...
.USED.LORIE..
PAR.MUIRFIELD
ALS.ANTE.NASA
KIT.NESS.TRAM
```

30

```
PHIL.CDI.TAGS
AARE.RIM.UCLA
WHOA.ESP.RTES
SANDRAHAYNIE.
..EAT.LEI....
GEORGE.ANNIKA
IAN...NEC....
GREENS.WAGGLE
.SIT.ESE.....
.OAKLANDHILLS.
HIFI.NAG.GARY
SLAM.CDE.ETON
TYRO.EAS.RENE
```

31

```
FETA █ HOT █ PLUS
IRAS █ AGE █ EELY
VALHALLA █ TMAN
ESK █ IVE █ DEANE
█ █ DDE █ NOR █ █
FRED █ WOO █ MAG
CURTISSTRANGE
CEE █ RAW █ FOOT
SOY █ BAR █ █ █
PAVIN █ PUP █ FLA
RAIN █ FAIRWAYS
OREG █ ETC █ AMOK
BETH █ EEK █ DENS
```

32

```
HASH █ BART █ PJS
ARIA █ EVER █ LUG
LILY █ MEMO █ ALT
DONNACAPONI █ █
█ ION █ PHD █ █
JONES █ █ YEARS
ANO █ █ █ RES
MEDIC █ EAGLE
NRA █ FAN █ █
OUTOFBOUNDS █
INK █ STAR █ ICER
RAE █ BRIT █ KING
ANS █ YALE █ AIDS
```

33

```
SSS █ STP █ MASSE
ACE █ HUR █ MITTS
LATROBE █ CRASS
ELIOT █ LOVED █
MENU █ AIR █ SLAB
█ NORMAN █ EBB
LEADER █ TOARMS
ARR █ ROBERT █
DATA █ WAD █ ORBS
█ WRIST █ SNORE
SPAIN █ HOLEOUT
OGLED █ EPA █ NCO
RALLY █ RAY █ EEN
```

34

```
BOD █ TEE █ CCLII
ELI █ OIL █ AHEAD
TIA █ LEE █ SIGNS
SOLHEIMCUP █ █
█ ADO █ MASHIE
FAZIO █ POL █ EVA
ONER █ SAN █ IRAS
RNA █ CAR █ FRONT
DELEON █ PRO █
█ JUDYRANKIN
PETER █ EEN █ IDO
ALECS █ NEC █ TOE
SLATE █ SNO █ ELS
```

35

```
FLAG █ BEAM █ FSU
LOSE █ RENI █ AER
AUSTRALIA █ RRS
█ TEE █ MARIA
AKRON █ TWIG █
TWO █ TORO █ RUST
IANBAKERFINCH
PISA █ LEMA █ UAE
█ CPAS █ TOMMY
LINKS █ RAF █
ABU █ HAZELTINE
KEN █ ALAN █ ECON
ETS █ WEPT █ NINE
```

36

```
BOSC █ PUSH █ BID
ARIA █ AROO █ ERA
MEGMALLON █ TAM
AGNEW █ NOSH █
█ OLEG █ RHETT
LIC █ SLED █ ESSO
ISLE █ UNO █ DDAY
MAUL █ LENO █ ARS
BOBBY █ STAB █
█ HEAR █ HOGAN
ADE █ BALTUSROL
BOA █ BITE █ NIKE
END █ ALDA █ STIR
```

37

```
SNOW █ ABC █ EPIC
LOLA █ REL █ AUTO
ATIT █ MAO █ GREG
WINSTONSALEM █
█ OSU █ ERE █ █
CORNER █ DESIGN
SAN █ █ █ NEO
TRAGIC █ WEDGES
█ EVA █ HOO █
█ LLOYDMANGRUM
LIAR █ DOL █ LORE
BERG █ INE █ ELSA
JUDE █ EAR █ GLAD
```

38

```
ATOM █ FDR █ BRAN
CHIC █ LEN █ RENO
ERNIEELS █ OATS
YUK █ SCI █ COREY
█ ASK █ OLD █ █
POOR █ TAU █ AAA
BUCKETOFBALLS
SIT █ VAN █ LPGA
█ RED █ FAS █ █
JAPAN █ RUN █ EBB
OPEN █ PARTHREE
USCG █ AMY █ OMAR
ROSE █ TSK █ TANG
```

39

```
STAB █ DRAG █ BUT
ORCA █ CORR █ LTS
PARR █ CLUE █ OAK
PEBBLEBEACH █
█ ELI █ ANS █ █
SPORT █ █ SHORT
EAR █ █ █ DEE
CRAIG █ █ STEVE
█ ALA █ CAR █
JANEBLALOCK █
BUS █ NEAR █ PHIL
ILK █ NAST █ HOLE
GIS █ AMTS █ YULE
```

40

```
MSS █ GPA █ DOZEN
ITA █ LEI █ ERODE
DENMARK █ EGEST
SNEAD █ MEDAL █
TORY █ PAM █ NLCS
█ BOUNCE █ ERE
HUBERT █ ESCROW
USO █ STPETE █
DABS █ ESS █ DRAT
█ HENRY █ BAUGH
DROVE █ CHARLIE
DUPER █ HAL █ ELS
EMEND █ OYL █ SEE
```

41

```
REF █ PCS █ DATES
ORO █ LOO █ ERATO
BIO █ AUS █ VIJAY
BETSYRAWLS █ █
█ SET █ AIELLO
BEARD █ PIN █ OID
ELMS █ GET █ NONO
LIE █ GAG █ PETER
LANGER █ PUB █
█ ROYALTROON
ATPAR █ MAT █ MAY
DOING █ ITE █ IRS
SWEDE █ NOR █ TSE
```

42

```
MAAM █ FRED █ DUD
PANE █ ANTI █ APO
GUNDERSON █ LOU
█ ITE █ EKING
PITCH █ JEDI █
UNO █ IGOR █ WAGS
FRANCISOUIMET
FETA █ VEST █ INA
█ RTES █ UNDER
ROCCO █ PRO █ █
ORO █ SORENSTAM
MEL █ KNOT █ ESTA
PGA █ ISEE █ YEAR
```

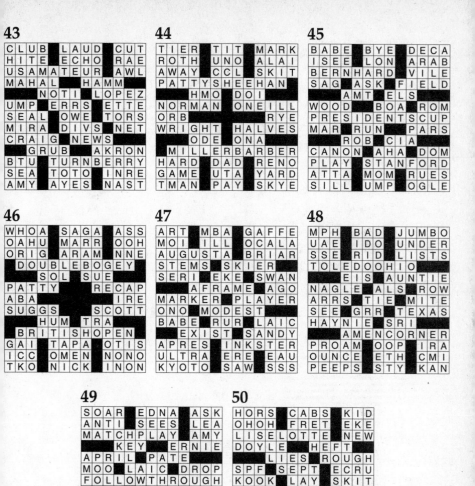

43

```
CLUB  LAUD  CUT
HITE  ECHO  RAE
USAMATEUR  AWL
MAHAL    HAMM
   NOTI  LOPEZ
UMP  ERRS  ETTE
SEAL  OWE  TORS
MIRA  DIVS  NET
CRAIG  NEWS
  GRUB   AKRON
BTU  TURNBERRY
SEA  TOTO  INRE
AMY  AYES  NAST
```

44

```
TIER  TIT  MARK
ROTH  UNO  ALAI
AWAY  CCL  SKIT
PATTYSHEEHAN
   HMO  DOI
NORMAN  ONEILL
ORB      RYE
WRIGHT  HALVES
   ODE  ONA
MILLERBARBER
HARD  DAD  RENO
GAME  UTA  YARD
TMAN  PAY  SKYE
```

45

```
BABE  BYE  DECA
ISEE  LON  ARAB
BERNHARD  VILE
SAG  ASK  FIELD
   AMT  ELS
WOOD   BOA  ROM
PRESIDENTSCUP
MAR  RUN  PARS
   ROB  CIA
CANON  AHA  DOM
PLAY  STANFORD
ATTA  MOM  RUES
SILL  UMP  OGLE
```

46

```
WHOA  SAGA  ASS
OAHU  MARR  OOH
ORIG  ARAM  NNE
 DOUBLEBOGEY
  SOL  SUE
PATTY    RECAP
ABA    IRE
SUGGS    SCOTT
  HUM  TRA
 BRITISHOPEN
GAI  TAPA  OTIS
ICC  OMEN  NONO
TKO  NICK  INON
```

47

```
ART  MBA  GAFFE
MOI  ILL  OCALA
AUGUSTA  BRIAR
STEMS  SKIER
SERI  EKE  SWAN
  AFRAME  AGO
MARKER  PLAYER
ONO  MODEST
BABE  RUR  LAIC
 EXIST  SANDY
APRES  INKSTER
ULTRA  ERE  EAU
KYOTO  SAW  SSS
```

48

```
MPH  BAD  JUMBO
UAE  IDO  UNDER
SSE  RID  LISTS
TOLEDOOHIO
   EIS  AUNTIE
NAGLE  ALS  ROW
ARRS  TIE  MITE
SEE  GRR  TEXAS
HAYNIE  SRI
  AMENCORNER
PROAM  OOP  IRA
OUNCE  ETH  CMI
PEEPS  STY  KAN
```

49

```
SOAR  EDNA  ASK
ANTI  SEES  LEA
MATCHPLAY  AMY
  KEY  ERNIE
APRIL  PATE
MOO  LAIC  DROP
FOLLOWTHROUGH
MLLE  ECTO  SRI
  MESH  CREEL
TULSA  ACE
ARE  GILMORGAN
PGA  LVII  UTAH
SEN  EYED  NEAL
```

50

```
HORS  CABS  KID
OHOH  FRET  EKE
LISELOTTE  NEW
DOYLE  HEFT
  LIES  ROUGH
SPF  SEPT  ECRU
KOOK  LAY  SKIT
YOUR  SIRS  YDS
ERROR  NECK
  SCAR  ONEUP
PRO  WHITWORTH
TOM  LONI  TIED
ADE  SSTS  SESS
```

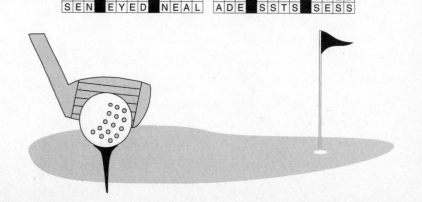